Following My Path

Striving for Justice and Social Change

Esther Maria Ritter

Edited by Judy Ann Ritter

LifeRich
PUBLISHING

LifeRich Publishing is a registered trademark of The Reader's Digest Association, Inc.

LifeRich Publishing books may be ordered through booksellers or by contacting:

LifeRich Publishing
1663 Liberty Drive
Bloomington, IN 47403
www.liferichpublishing.com
1 (888) 238-8637

ISBN: 978-1-4897-2580-6 (sc)
ISBN: 978-1-4897-2582-0 (hc)
ISBN: 978-1-4897-2581-3 (e)

Library of Congress Control Number: 2019920666

Print information available on the last page.

LifeRich Publishing rev. date: 12/17/2019

Dedication

To Jan Swenson-She got me in touch with Ray and shared my interest in Central America.

To Ray Plankey-He helped me find a place in Mexico to live, and always treated me as if my disability was secondary. I also want to thank him for all his support. I often called him my guardian angel.

To Sonia Garcia—She understood my lifelong dream to visit Nicaragua and helped to find a school where I could live while I improved my Spanish.

Maria de La Paz-A special thanks to my adorable godchild, who brought light, laughter, and love into my life.

Contents

Editor's Acknowledgments

I WOULD LIKE to thank my Write-on-Group in Sturgeon Bay, Wisconsin, for their help reading some of the chapters and giving advice for improvement.

A special thanks to my husband, Markus Ritter, for helping with the housework so I could work on his sister's book. I also commend him for the excellent technical help he provided, a techy I am not.

A well-deserved acknowledgment to Peter Ritter, Regina Beatus, and Ruth Cakans, Esther's siblings, for their help in providing journals, letters, pictures, and encouragement.

Ruth Cakans deserves a special thanks for last-minute editing.

Without all this help, this book would not exist.

Introduction

I LOVED TO sail. Because I couldn't afford to join the Hoofer's Sailing Club at the University of Wisconsin, I ran out on the pier whenever I saw a lone sailor. "Do you need a crew?" I would ask.

"Sure," said a blond, blue-eyed sailor with a delightful smile.

So I jumped onto the bow of the tech dingy and knocked us both into the fresh spring waters of Lake Mendota. I was sure I would never hear from him again.

But right after Easter vacation, there was a note from him on my dorm door. We started dating, and that is how I met the Ritter family—the father, Henry; the mother, Heidi; Markus, the guy I dunked and later married; Peter, the younger brother; Esther, the narrator of this story; and Ruth and Regina, the two younger sisters.

During my visit, I learned more about the family. The Ritter family emigrated from Switzerland, coming to America in 1949. Mr. Ritter was a minister, who concluded people should enter baptism as adults, not as babies. The Swiss Church required he not discuss his beliefs concerning adult baptism. He felt that one should only get baptized when aware of what baptism meant. He would not deny his convictions; so, he could not enter its service.

When he was recovering from polio in a St. Gallen Hospital in Switzerland in 1931, he learned of a spiritualist named John Keller. After many years of theological education, he was offered a position with a small group of John Keller's followers in Chicago who needed a minister. The Ritter family was required to wait four years for a Visa to enter the United States. After preparing, he packed up his family and their belongings in 1949 and sailed on the Queen Elizabeth to America, where he hoped for freedom of religion to preach his true beliefs.

The Ritter family

The Ritter family worked and lived on a farm in Grafton owned by their sponsor. After a year, Mr. Ritter and his wife bought a farm and moved to Oak Creek. When the freeway cut the property in half in 1959, they moved to a ranch house, where I met the family.

Esther and I were closest in age, Esther being only four months younger than me. I sensed right away; she was an intelligent person who had thoughts different from my own. She speculated about the world at large. Hung up on passing tests and enjoying life with minimal worries concerning politics or what our government was doing in the world, I guess you would call me naive. Esther opened my eyes; the United States wasn't always right, and there were worldwide consequences to our government's actions.

Her high school diaries reveal a normal insecure teenage girl who likes boys. She strategizes how she needs to change her looks and behavior to attract particular ones. She stresses how she must not chase them, must keep her respectability, but still have them pursue her.

She seemed to want to be in the popular group but regrets giving up her individual beliefs and freedoms to be part of that group.

To search for the roots of her activism, I scanned her diaries. There were notes from a book she read, Little Bit by Eve Bennet. "Everybody is a person and wants to live a full life. Don't be with the mighty and forget the commoners. Don't think only of yourself and doing better than others. Put yourself in their shoes. Share their joys and sorrows." Esther wrote this in her diary the summer before going to college at UW Eau Claire, Wisconsin, in 1961.

After seeing the movie Ben Hur, Esther wrote in her journal, "The scenes of the lepers in the dungeons left their mark. In the valley of the lepers, they lived in caves like animals. That movie makes one remember today that some people still need help."

These were the seeds that sprouted, grew deep roots, and supported Esther's lifelong thirst for knowledge and her accompanying activism.

When Esther died on October 1, 2005, she left behind the beginning of a memoir. Her family gave me her diaries, journals, and tapes made when she could no longer write with her hands. I, Esther's sister-in-law, promised to edit and complete her book. The result, Following My Path: Striving for Justice and Social Change, is the story of a woman who, at thirty-eight, received a devastating diagnosis. Sharing her experiences, she wanted to give hope to others facing the same future for a full life.

Help

I AM IN the spare bedroom, hibernating inside because of the icy winter blasts in Wisconsin. Today there was a blizzard, and tonight I had to change bedrooms because of the howling north winds, which shook the windowpanes, and I couldn't sleep.

It is nights like this when my mind drifts to fantasies of living in sunny Mexico, which warms my soul. I imagine the tropic sun tanning my skin while stretching out on the beach, with gentle salty sea breezes blowing in from the Pacific Ocean. I can almost smell the spicy Mexican cooking and taste the juicy tangerines bursting on my tongue with their heavenly sweetness. Laughing children surround me, singing songs, and townspeople stop to say hola and send smiles my way.

Then I wake up in this dreary room with the gloomy dark blue-colored walls, alone once again. The people I meet in Mineral Point, Wisconsin, are social workers, psychologists, and a few friends when they aren't too busy. I don't want the isolating impersonal social services to be my life; I need friends with similar interests. Being handicapped is not my primary focus in life.

In my early thirties, I joined a commune in the New Hampshire wilds called The Wooden Shoe. We planted and harvested crops, prepared meals, and comforted and argued with each other the way other families do. As work crews, we toiled on the land to make money needed for raw materials or items we couldn't make.

After three years, I left to see where life might take me next. Joining the members of the Clamshell Alliance of Environmental Groups, I protested and blocked the construction of a nuclear power plant in Seabrook, New Hampshire. The police jailed us in an old National Guard armory for our efforts. But this started the grassroots antinuclear movement, and we were proud. Yes, I was a gypsy, but I was a gypsy with a cause.

By the 1980s, I was having problems with balance. I was unsteady using stairs. Helping my nephew learn to ride a bike, I ran along beside him but kept falling. I remembered ice-skating with my friends in California in 1979, but when I visited Boston just three years later and tried to skate, my legs vibrated so much I couldn't keep them steady. Even when walking downhills, I had to concentrate on taking each step.

My attempt to swim was the last straw. When swimming underwater, I breathed through my nose, got water into my trachea, and came up gasping for air. Flailing my arms, I made it to the pool edge. I tried again, first taking deep breaths and holding my breath as I dove. But the same thing happened again. I had no control over breathing in the water. Jumping into the pool holding my nose worked, but I hadn't needed to do that since I was little and first learned how to swim. I remember diving off rafts without even thinking about breathing. My symptoms were getting worse, and I wondered why. Could I have a brain tumor interfering with my thought-action patterns?

I consulted a neurologist at a nearby hospital.

"After listening to your symptoms, I believe you should have some tests," he said.

My insurance would pay, but a CT scan of the brain with a contrasting dye and a myelogram, including a spinal tap, wasn't what I expected. Yikes! Speechless for a moment, I tried to gain control. "Okay, when?" I whispered.

"The nurse will be in to set up a date for the tests," he said.

The tests were painful, but when they were over, I heaved a sigh of relief. Then came the hardest part—the waiting. One morning, the phone rang, and I rushed to answer it.

"I have the results of your test," the doctor said. "With your symptoms, I'm sure something is wrong with your nervous system, but it's too early for our tests to detect it yet. We can do them again in six months to a year."

I comprehended little else he said. Oh, great, all that fear and pain, and I'm back to square one!

Meeting An Alternative Doctor

WHEN THE NEUROLOGIST wasn't able to diagnose a disease, it discouraged me. I needed to fight against a condition with a name. I wanted a second opinion. Shrinks always detected something, but not something physical.

"What do you believe is the problem?" they'd asked me.

Their questioning me in this way made me wonder if it was only faulty thinking on my part. My psychologist said she didn't understand me, and it is seldom she doesn't; she always can help her clients.

I wasn't trying to be hard to figure out. I couldn't figure myself out sometimes. My life was full of bizarre, disruptive events. The moment I believed I was doing okay, wham, an experience hit me and blew it apart. It left me trying to pick up the pieces.

I decided it was time to seek an alternative doctor and discovered one from India. She received her degree from Edinburgh, Scotland, and has practiced for thirty years. Over the last six years, she shifted to an alternative approach.

"What do you think of me spending money on another opinion?" I asked my mother.

My thrifty mother spoke about a woman who spent $70,000 on doctors and had to cure herself of cancer via the "Grape Cure." My mother tried, but these isolated success stories didn't help. I wondered how many individuals were not cured; you never heard about them.

"What if you aren't better after treatments?" Mother asked.

"What if I am?" I replied.

The alternative doctor tested me with an electro-acupuncture machine developed by Dr. Voll in Germany. It uses electronic sensors to measure excesses and deficiencies along the acupuncture meridians. The device looked like something Leonardo da Vinci might have imagined. I gripped onto an antenna in one hand. The doctor used a probe that looked like a blunt knitting needle. She moved it around my fingers and toes and read the results on a dial. She diagnosed me with severe hypoglycemia and some nervous system inflammation.

"You will need to eat six times a day, high protein, low starch, and nibble some protein every two hours. This will keep your blood sugar at normal levels," she said. "I also recommend you abstain from coffee and other caffeinated drinks."

Adhering to the diet for a month, I didn't get as suicidal, hopeless, or worried about my future as I had a month ago. My symptoms seemed to diminish. I'd waited so long for some improvement. Not wanting to be disappointed, I followed my doctor's advice to the letter, not a drop of coffee or caffeinated soda, only water and peppermint tea. My brain was brighter, and I'd been sleeping better. Wasn't this worth the $100 spent so far?

Now What?

3

BUT BY 1985, I wasn't feeling well again, so I made an appointment for another test. The results were worse. Instead of an inflamed nervous system, I now had degeneration of the brain stem. My hypoglycemic condition was closer to diabetes.

The doctor spoke softly, trying to comfort me. "I'm sorry, but with the results of the test and your symptoms of weakness, poor balance, slurring of words, and tripping when walking, I would diagnose you in the early stages of ALS," she said.

I didn't know much about ALS, except that others named it Lou Gehrig's disease after the Yankee baseball player who was diagnosed with it.

"It is a progressive disease where your nerves degenerate and cause muscle weakness, paralysis, and respiratory failure," she said. "When elderly people get the disease, they usually die within five years. But for younger people like yourself, you could live another twenty years."

I'm not getting better? Only progressively worse? I walked around in a daze for a few weeks, not feeling anything but shock. When I let the diagnosis into my consciousness, I must admit, I thought of suicide. The helplessness just overwhelmed me. How can I live knowing that each year, I will lose another function?

Eventually, I remembered I could live another twenty years. Might some of my dreams come true? At this crossroad, I could either give up or continue the life I wanted to live, disability, or not. I did not want to spend my winters in my mother's home with the depressing dark blue walls and frigid Wisconsin temperatures. Someplace warm sounded good—someplace with a kindred community where I could be useful while still able.

My friend, Jan, called to see how I was. I told her how devastated I was and about my diagnosis.

"Oh, Esther. I'm so sorry. But remember—you still have twenty years," Jan said, always the optimist. "Maybe this will make you feel better. I called for another reason. I have learned of a center in Cuernavaca, Mexico, where people can find out how they can help the poor," Jan said. "I believe, with your experiences with the grassroots movement, this might be just what you need."

"Thank you for giving me some hope, Jan," I said. "You always do."

I asked my mother to drive me to the Mineral Point Library to do some research. A hundred-year-old building in downtown Mineral Point on Front Street houses the library, which initially served as a church. Although the steps in front were clear of snow, I had a difficult time using my walker when climbing the stairs. If I hung onto the railing and pulled myself step by step up the stairs, I could manage. Mother brought the walker to the top of the front steps. "I'll be back in about an hour," she said.

There were several books on Mexico and one with an entire chapter on Cuernavaca. I learned Cuernavaca, the City of Eternal Spring, is the capital city of Mexico's Morelos state. It lies fifty miles south of Mexico City. Wow, sounds good. No winter, only spring! The lowest temperature is about 66 degrees, and the warmest 74 degrees, while Wisconsin can get below zero in winter and over 90 degrees in the summer.

Perhaps the pace of life would be slower than the hustle and bustle of living in the United States. Maybe I need a more leisurely pace because my life seems to be ebbing away with this terrible disease. If I just slow down, perhaps my life will last longer. I knew I was grasping at straws, but what does one do with such a diagnosis?

The warmer temperatures would give me more energy, and to learn about a new culture where I might become part of a movement would be exciting. Cuernavaca would be much healthier for me. But in the back of my mind, I wondered, will they accept me and my disability?

Writing a Letter

4

ON JANUARY 10, 1987, I wrote the founder of the Cuernavaca Center:

Dear Mr. Plankey,

I learned about you and the Cuernavaca Center for Intercultural Dialogue on Development (CCIDD) from a friend of mine. She shares my interest in Central America and Mexico.

I am writing to ask if you could help me find a place to live in Cuernavaca with a Mexican family who might like to assist a disabled person to live in Mexico. I receive a Social Security disability check ($289/month). I would be more than willing to share it with a family in a mutually beneficial way.

My interest in peace and social justice directed me to become an

9

activist in various organizations. I find much hope in the liberation theology interpretation of the Bible, both for my personal struggle and the broader fight for social change. It is my hope I may take part in the community where your center is if only a few hours a week. I wish to maintain continuity with the direction my life was taking before my disability.

I have Lou Gehrig's disease, a degenerative disease affecting the nerves and causing atrophy of the muscles, especially in my hands and calf muscles. My first symptoms began in 1980, and I've been coping with its insidious effects ever since. I function much better in a warm climate.

Two years ago, I used a cane, today I use a walker, and perhaps soon I will need a wheelchair. I can take care of my personal needs, except I move slowly. Although, when on my knees with knee pads, I move fast.

Shopping and laundry are two activities with which I would need considerable help. I love to cook, and a diet of frequent frijoles does not bother me because legumes are a regular part of my diet now.

Mr. Plankey, I hope my disability does not scare you. I am capable, resourceful, and even creative in coping with my problems and new situations.

My impression is third world people are more at ease with disabilities than middle-class Americans.

I am living with my sixty-nine-year-old mother, who thank God, is in good health. We live in a small middle-class town in rural Wisconsin. If I stay here, I foresee more isolation in my future, not only because of my disability but also because of my interests.

An indoor toilet would be essential because of my disability. If my social security check is not enough, my family has offered to supplement it. My mother relies on social security, as well. I've learned some Spanish and could live with a family who speaks little or no English.

Mr. Plankey, I have prayed to find a contact and a place as politically aware as your center. I hope you may contact a family with whom I may live, even if only for a month or two, although I wish my stay to be much longer.

Enclosed is a check for $25, which should cover a ten-minute phone call if you would be so kind as to phone me at your convenience. If we talk for over ten minutes, I will call you back. If you prefer to write, fine. Please keep the check as a donation.

Thank you for any help you can give.

Esther Maria Ritter

5

Ray

I DIDN'T HEAR from Mr. Plankey for many months and believed maybe I never would. His center must keep him busy. Most of my immediate family thought I was crazy, out of my mind. My mother didn't put it in those terms, but I worried her.

"Esther, you might get into trouble, and being so far away in Mexico," Mother said, "How could I help you? Here, in Mineral Point, health care and social workers can help you handle your symptoms."

"The rest of my life is all I have," I told her. "I will trust in God and follow my dreams." I explained I had written a letter for help to find a place in Cuernavaca, Mexico, and hoped to hear soon. Nothing could stop me. But why hadn't Ray called?

Early one morning, the phone rang, and I thought it was for my mother, as her friends often telephoned in the morning.

"Hello. May I please speak with Esther?" a man's voice asked.

"Yes, this is she," I replied.

"This is Ray Plankey," he said. "I put your letter on a bulletin board at the center and have received two responses—one a single woman and the other a family. Are you still interested in coming for a visit?"

"Yes, yes, as soon as I can arrange a flight," I said.

"I'm glad," Ray said. "I'm looking forward to meeting you."

"Me too," I said. "I will tell you when I plan to arrive. You don't know how much this means to me, Ray," I added. "Thank you so much. I'll be in touch soon."

"You're welcome. Goodbye, Esther."

Every time I saw my reflection in a mirror, there was a smile and a look of relief.

After planning with the airline, I called Ray on my arrival time. I saw him waving as the crew helped me disembark. Relishing the warm weather, I took off my sweater and then my shoes and my socks. I wouldn't wear socks in Mexico since then; the weather was perfect.

We drove up over the mountains on the non-toll road, which wound through a village or two. We got stuck behind a huge truck that splashed water out each time it went over a bump.

"Why are water trucks up high in the mountains?" I asked Ray.

"Many of the independent farmers up here can't afford the money for irrigation," he said. "They depend on the water trucks to sustain their crops."

Driving higher into the mountains, we passed a few of these farms. Around the curve was a low valley surrounded by pine forests and acres of yellow oat shocks waiting for the harvest.

"Oh, how lovely!" I said.

"Yes, this is one of my favorite areas," Ray answered. "I enjoy seeing it whenever I drive this way."

I wished this ride would never end. Compared to the winter I'd left behind in Wisconsin, this was paradise. I felt so alive and hopeful, not depressed, not focusing on my disease.

We arrived much too soon in Cuernavaca.

"Esther, you may stay at CCIDD for the evening," Ray said. "I'll pick you up tomorrow morning so we can check out the two places I've found for you to live."

I stayed in one of the rooms at the center with the windows wide open, so the soft breezes cooled me while I slept. With such a busy day, I had no trouble falling asleep.

The next morning, a colorful platter of juicy citrus fruits sat on the breakfast table, along with bowls of granola, raisins, and nuts, which reminded me of muesli, the cereal of my youth when I lived in Switzerland.

After I finished eating, Ray came. "Ready to go?" he asked.

"Yes, I'm excited," I replied.

Ray wheeled me out to the car, settled me into the front seat, and put the wheelchair in the trunk.

"The first place is in a nice section of town," he said.

I could see that as soon as we turned the corner onto a tree-lined, shady street with stately kept yards and many houses built behind solid walls. Here we met a woman named Camila, who showed us her home. "I'll include a private bath with your bedroom," she said as she opened the door.

The first thing I noticed was a French door and a green lawn with colorful patches of a variety of flowers, bushes, and tall shade trees. The light poured into the room. What a lovely place to live, I thought.

Camila offered us lemonade as we sat around the kitchen table. After she poured the lemonade into three glasses, she lit up a cigarette. Uh-oh, a red flag. I had just spent an up-and-down year trying to quit, and I didn't need the temptation. Four cats wandered throughout the house, and I didn't want them in my room either. Camila also lived alone, so I wondered what help I could expect.

Ray sensed my hesitation. "We have another place to check out today," he said. "We will let you know sometime tomorrow."

"Camila, what a charming home you have," I said. "Thank you for showing it to us.

Back in the car, I explained to Ray my hesitation, and he said he understood.

In the afternoon, we drove up to the driveway of the other possibility. This house was not in as grand a section of town—no formal gardens or protective walls—but it was near the center.

Sylvia, the lady of the house, invited us for lunch. We ate rice, beans, and tortillas filled with pork simmered in spices. After lunch, Sylvia showed us the room. It was right across from the bathroom. The walls were bright fuchsia, but the curtains were a lovely pale pink covered with flowers. I worried about the constant traffic to the bathroom outside the room. Although I expected this, the owners had warned me; I thought there would be a door. I needed privacy, so I asked Sylvia if she had another room with a door.

"Yes, at the end of the hall," Sylvia said.

This place had sunny yellow walls, such a cheerful place to live.

"This is perfect," I said.

"My husband and our four children plus my mother live

with us," Sylvia explained. "Someone will be here when you need help."

Here, I have a lifeline to the world outside—a phone, a real telephone with a cord, which would allow me to call Ray at the center, and my family and friends at home.

6

The Cuernavaca Center for Intercultural Dialogue on Development (CCIDD)

"THE PRIMARY REASON I came to Mexico was this center," I told Ray, asking, "What is the main goal of this center?"

"We offer Canadian and American citizens the opportunity to experience the struggle for justice in Latin America," Ray said.

"I came to Cuernavaca to live and continue to study liberation theology," I replied. "I am hoping to contribute while I am still able."

At one of the liberation theology meetings, I learned help implies inequality; one side is stronger than the other. Service, however, is a relationship between equals.

"You could serve by starting a cross-cultural dialogue, or maybe you could work in the garden," Ray explained.

I know being close to this center will be vital to me. In my liberation theology class, I learned the movement, which was established in the 1950s, was a reaction to poverty and social injustice in Latin America. The principle was that committing oneself to service to improve the lives of the oppressed would result in ultimate salvation.

The Vatican disliked identifying the Catholic Church of South America as members of the privileged class that had been oppressing indigenous populations for a long time.

"Tomorrow, nine North Americans from various churches are coming to CCIDD to visit," Ray said. "They are not coming as tourists and staying at a fancy hotel but will live at the center. They will visit with people and learn how they live. The goal is to improve their quality of life.

"Esther, I would like you to lead the tour tomorrow," Ray asked me. "You know enough Spanish to help interpret. How about it?"

"Sure, it would give me a chance to practice my Spanish," I said. In my heart, I felt I belonged here, and I was happy to contribute.

7

Patios de la Estación

THE NORTH AMERICAN Christian group gathered in the meeting hall for an introduction by Ray before we walked together to the Patios de la Estación—the railroad station yard's settlement. "The abandoned railroad station yards are only a few blocks from this center. The residents built shelters, and so far, the government has not made them move," Ray said. "In some other cities, the government bulldozed them down.

"Esther will be your guide and interpreter today," Ray added, gesturing to me. "She knows the way."

One of the members held out his hand to me. "Hi, Esther. My name is Robert," he said. "I will push you in your wheelchair if you like."

"Thank you. I do get tired, so I would appreciate that when we get to the settlement," I said. "The dirt pathways can be rough."

As we walked on the smooth walkways from the center, Patios de la Estación appeared without warning. Instead of busy city streets, cardboard shacks and huts made of twigs began to appear.

I needed help in some narrow areas, rolling over small logs and crossing a rickety bridge over a creek of soapy water. Bright white clothes were drying on clotheslines outside many of the shacks. The contrasting smells of raw sewage and food cooking mixed together, making us queasy.

The North Americans and the residents of the settlement helped me so I could go inside some dwellings to interpret when the people talked about their lives. They told of the Base Christian Community, a grassroots organization that served them by trying to organize to get better conditions like water and electricity.

"Many people come from the country to live in the city to find work, like cleaning or doing people's laundry. Their children wash windshields out on the street for a hundred pesos, about eighteen cents," I explained to the group. "What I mean when I say wash windshields is when you stop your car, a little boy or girl will wash your windshield, hoping you will give them something before the light turns green again. Please watch out for these children."

In this settlement, people lived with dirt paths, no running water, and crowded conditions.

I interpreted. "I clean the houses of wealthy people. I moved here with my husband and children last January from a mountainous region where we didn't have enough good food to eat," one woman said. "Often we ate only corn and beans, which wasn't good for the children.

"Living in the mountains away from the major cities is hard in the winter because we can't grow our food without irrigation, which is too expensive. Crops only grow in the rainy season from May to December," she continued. "The rest of the year we must go to the bigger cities, where we can find work and buy our food. I also weave baskets and embroider clothes to sell at the local farmer's market, and they sell better in larger cities like this one."

As we were leaving, we all said, "Gracias," together. I noticed that, although the people were poor, they brought beauty into their lives by planting flowers in old coffee tins and growing other decorative plants, no matter how small their plot of land. Another woman invited us into her home, which was the size of an average living room with one swinging bare light bulb to brighten the interior. Pictures of smiling children torn from calendars decorated the walls. A cross, fashioned out of paper-mâché, occupied the space above the table.

The woman told us in Spanish (I interpreted again), "We can get water at the park, but it flows only a few times a day, and we must haul it to where we live. My shelter has a gas stove so I can heat water for bathing or cooking. I am lucky. Most of my friends don't have stoves, so sometimes they heat water on my stove. We help each other when we can."

The group visited another place where the people lived in worse conditions. Cuernavaca is a city built around ravines where development is not possible. Destitute people live there. I couldn't visit this area; I would need to be carried, which would be too risky.

When the group returned to the bus, anyone could see on their faces how affected they were. With teary eyes, they entered and sat quietly, deep in thought.

The next morning, one participant asked Ray, "How can God allow this to happen?"

"Many others have asked me that question," Ray replied.

"Maybe this is not your question to God but God's question to you?"

The group promised to collect money and clothing at their churches to help improve the conditions for the people they had met. This was our goal, so this was a successful trip, and I felt like an activist again.

In the afternoon, we visited the market in the rural village of Tepoztian, about half an hour from Cuernavaca. On the ride, we saw acres and acres of roses growing in the fields. The market had a festive atmosphere, where the indigenous people sold produce, flowers, garments, handicrafts, and jewelry. Women in colorful dresses often carried their infants in their shawls strapped over their backs or in front of them. The group enjoyed the atmosphere and bought several items to support the sellers and bring home to family and friends. I purchased whole grain rice, which I can't find in Cuernavaca. Sylvia loves roses, and she does so much for me; she deserves something special, so I bought a dozen red roses for her.

Tomorrow the group will leave, and I am going with my "Mexican family" on an outing they planned.

8

My Mexican Family

I AM EXPERIENCING living with a Mexican family. Sylvia, the woman of the house, is an excellent cook and makes healthy yet tasty food. Her husband, Pablo, works as an upholstery apprentice and is doing well. Sylvia also supplements the household with her earnings as a Tupperware lady. Their oldest daughter, Magdalena, twenty-five, doesn't live at home. Their son, Carlos, is twenty; Louisa, nineteen, attends beauty school; Anna Maria is eighteen, and nine-year-old Juanita completes the family. Juanita often runs to the little stand down the street for my favorite lime-roasted squash seeds, always with a smile; she is a happy, delightful girl.

Their grandmother, Maria, lives with us. She was born in Acapulco and now owns a little store on the street, where she sells clothing and comic books. Their great-grandmother lives in the rural area outside Cuernavaca.

My Mexican family took me along when they visited her today. She lives in an adobe house with a yard, a few fruit trees, flowers, berry bushes, and enough space for the chickens to roam.

"Great-grandmother, this is Esther, our friend living with us now," Juanita said. "Esther, this is Juanita. I have her name to honor her," Juanita said.

"Nice to meet you, Juanita," I said. "I enjoy living with your family. They are always willing to help me, especially your namesake," I said.

"I'm sure her parents raised her that way," Great-Grandma said.

"My late husband and I used to farm this land, growing rows of corn and plowing the ground with horses we owned," she said. When she spoke of her husband, she looked at the empty chair as if he were sitting across the table from us. Her eyes were brimming with tears as she told me, "He was so tall and handsome, and his gray eyes sparkled when I gazed into them. When I lost him, I couldn't think of marrying again. He was corazón mio" (my heart).

We talked about life and its curves, and I told her about my disease and the reasons I had come to Cuernavaca. I always have something in common with people who know death isn't too far away—a commonality that transcends culture, language, and geography.

9

Seeing a Curandero

MY MEXICAN FAMILY became engaged with helping me live a better life, making healthy foods, and taking me for walks in the fresh air. They encouraged me to visit a curandero or healer. I'm not sure about this, but it can't hurt to try something new.

Sylvia and Pablo don't own a car, so I hired a cab. The cab bumped along an old dirt road full of potholes and entered a muddy field where we parked. Sylvia's husband, and Carlos, their son, took me in the wheelchair a quarter of a mile up a stony path.

Once, we stopped for a herd of seventy to eighty goats, which smelled like dirty clothes, left unwashed for a while. Goats of all ages and colors reminded me of my childhood home. Our family kept a small group, and I remembered milking them as a child.

When we got to the gate, we joined native women waiting for the curandero; he had not arrived yet. Across the road, I saw piglets playing and squealing in the mud like little children who'd just found out how much fun puddles can be. A wall surrounded the curandero's house; most people with any money build a wall around their home.

The healer opened the gate because we had made an appointment. Sylvia rolled me into his office. "I'll go with you for support," she said.

A table stood next to the bed. A glass of water and a plastic object that looked like a dresser drawer knob sat on top.

"I can see in the water what's wrong with you and measure your energy with this crystal," he said as he held up the knob. "If you give me 400,000 pesos, I can heal you right now."

I looked at Sylvia, and she rolled her eyes.

"No," I replied. "That is absurd, I can't afford that much."

When we told the cab driver what had happened, he said, "I know of another curandero who lives in Queretaro, about half an hour away. He is cheaper and, I believe, more honest."

We tried one more time. When we arrived at the second curandero's house, Sylvia knocked on the door.

"He is not here but in his fields in the country. I'm sure he will want to help," his wife said. "I am cooking our evening meal, so he should come home soon."

She gave us instructions, and we found him sowing seeds in a plowed field a few miles from town. What a kind face he had. With graying hair, he looked about sixty years old.

We went to the house of the second healer, and again, Pablo and Carlos carried me over a concrete barrier at the gate. Sylvia rolled me into a shed at the back of his home. In the middle of the room was a double bed. A picture of Mary cradling her baby Jesus hung on the wall. A trestle arch covered with paper flowers stood in the room's corner. Was it carried during fiesta days? I wondered.

A variety of glass jars with fabric flowers sat on shelves. Someone had piled small ceramic and larger clay vases in a box. Were these gifts patients brought, hoping that the healer could cure them? Lots of religious items, including a picture of Guadalupe and a multitude of candles, decorated the room. A short table on the far right held a glass filled with water, a candle, and a dish with an egg. An exquisitely carved stone vessel sat in front. I stayed seated in my chair.

"You should lie down on the bed," Sylvia remarked.

The curandero opened the door. "Hello, Esther. I want you to know I am an honest man. My reputation is important to me. Therefore, I tell you ahead of time that I charge 5,000 pesos for this healing," he said. "Do you agree with this price?"

"Sí," I responded. What a difference! Five thousand pesos is about $2.50.

He poured a liquid from the stone vessel. "Our priest in our town blessed this; it is holy oil," he explained. He rubbed some on my forehead. Crossing over my chest, he invoked the name of the Father, the Son, and the Holy Ghost.

Next, the curandero rolled the egg over my eyes, my face, and around my neck. "Let me help you sit up straighter so I can do your back," he said. Gently he took my hand and put his arm behind my back to help me sit. He moved the egg down my back and arms. But he didn't do much with my hands, even though they are not well. My feet are more deformed than my hands, so I suppose he decided my hands didn't need as much attention. He moved down my chest rubbing me with the egg and praying that the evil spirits would leave my body. I just prayed that it didn't break and get all over my clothes. I didn't like him touching my breast but said nothing because he moved on and proceeded down my body.

The curandero placed the egg on my navel and prayed for the longest time. He also spent several minutes on my legs and feet. After he finished, he was spinning around, shaking his hands.

When I looked at Sylvia and shrugged my shoulders, she realized I didn't understand. "I've had my share of massages," she said. "They shake their hands afterward and wash them with soap to dispel the negative energy."

The exciting thing was that, when the healer cracked the egg opened into the glass of water and examined it with a candle, the strangest thing happened in my mind. I felt spiritual energy going from my hand into the egg.

"This is all I can do for you today," the curandero explained. "There's a medicine that might help more."

"How much?" I asked.

"About 50,000 pesos," he replied.

Although that is only about $25, I can't afford it.

"Well, eat healthy foods. And if you find this cleansing helped you, I will do another for the same price," he said. "Adios, Esther. I wish you well."

"Gracias," I answered, and Sylvia rolled me to the cab.

I must admit today I had a bunch of energy and even bathed myself and washed clothes out by hand, which I rarely can do. Was there anything to this healing process? I wasn't sure, but I would not pay a whole load of money.

North American culture influences Mexico, yet the Mexican people are still in touch with their indigenous beliefs. Take, for example, the curandero, who said prayers and crossed himself in the name of the Father, the Son, and the Holy Ghost. He co-opted Catholicism into his culture with the rubbing of the egg. That was what he had done, and it didn't bother me in the least. So what? The man was a native. From where did his belief in this healing come? Not from Rome or Italy. Was it a scam? All I could do was draw on my sensations and experiences to test whatever happened.

Sylvia mentioned this morning how much better I seemed and is encouraging me to do more healings. If they are only 5,000 pesos apiece, I'll go ahead with them.

Someday, a weird thing may come out of the egg, and someone will have rigged it. My life is crazy some times, but as long as I keep it all in an analytical light, I'll be fine. Causes and effects exist in the spiritual world, just as in the physical one. All we can do is learn about them through our experiences and those of others. There is rationality in reality.

The curandero mentioned how maybe my mother or father might have affected me to cause my disease. I didn't understand that until this morning when Sylvia discussed it with me. I admit I have had more trouble and misunderstandings with my mother.

"That's what he said. It might be one of your parents," Sylvia explained.

"My father and I had an excellent relationship," I said. "It is not fair to blame anyone; my mother might have issues of her own."

Indigenous people of Mexico think a person gets sick because somebody does these things to them; I don't. No one knows what caused my disease, but I'm sure it had nothing to do with my mother or father. Someday scientists will find the cause, and a cure will not be far away. But it will be too late for me. So meanwhile, I must continue to live my life to the fullest.

10

Going to Oaxaca

TODAY I WENT to Oaxaca with Ray to meet with a group of indigenous women trying to form an organization that will help them. In Cuernavaca, the women learned to cut out the middleman and keep more of the profit for themselves. Today, I will explain how the Oaxacan women can create one too. I felt so useful and happy when I could contribute like this.

Waiting for Ray, I could look between trees and buildings to the mountain range going toward the south over which we will be driving. I could even see El Popo when it was a bright day like today. Popo is short for Popocatépet, which comes from the Nahuatl words popokal (it smokes) and tepetl (mountain); this describes a volcano to perfection.

Ray arrived and helped me into the front seat and stored my wheelchair in the back. As we ascended into the mountains, we saw peasants in the fields and their cattle loose along the road. The children tended the animals to prevent them from eating corn, beans, and squash. We observed one little boy yelling and waving his hands to scare a cow from entering the field. "Without fences, this is a steady job for the children,"

Ray said. "Notice the woman sitting under that tree weaving a hat."

"She must be used to all the yelling," I said. "She's oblivious to it all."

Many of the mountains had trees on them and often a cornfield with a hut on top of the hill. A herd of white goats roamed, grazing up and down the hill. Unfettered horses trotted along the roadside, and people rode others. Horses and burros are a primary form of transportation for the people. A little boy and girl rode bareback on a burro. "With all these people and animals on the side of the road," I said, "it is important to drive with caution as we do in Wisconsin to avoid a deer unexpectedly jumping out on the road."

Bus transportation must be available between major cities because we saw a bus stop sign in one village. I was sure many people had taken it when they could afford it.

The road to Oaxaca was in a superior condition. "You don't have to worry about frost here, so the pavement doesn't deteriorate as it would in Wisconsin," I said to Ray.

"Yes, but the curvy roads, and climbing these mountain ranges is a challenge," Ray answered.

Here and there, we would travel through a village where churches were the main buildings. "What magnificent churches so high in these mountains," I said.

"Yes, a sign of how important religion is here in these mountainous areas," Ray replied.

At this time of the year in Mexico, everything was lush because it is the rainy season. Oaxaca reminded me of a European city with a central square and a bandstand where a military band played patriotic music. A few restaurants lined the street, and there was a hotel, from which poured native tunes. Shady trees and brilliant fragrant flowers spread across the square. The music coming from the hotel drew us inside to find a folk dancing presentation.

The folk dancers were dressed in the costumes of their regions. The first group danced the Mexican hat dance. For this dance, the women wore a dress with a high collar decorated with colorful ribbons. Their skirts were long and had the same types of ribbons on the bottom. The men had a mariachi costume, a three-piece suit including a jacket with decorative silver buttons, a vest, a pair of pants, and a Mexican hat.

A single young lady from the Jalisco region of Mexico danced next. She wore a colorful dress with a wide circular skirt and decorative ribbon stripes of red, Mexican pink, yellow, and blue that formed a star. More of the colorful stripes decorated the bottom. She held the edge of her skirt and moved her hands back and forth with such grace that she created an exquisite rainbow effect as she stomped her feet and twirled.

We met with a Base Christian Community in Oaxaca on a lake. A woman called the barefoot doctor was teaching the indigenous villagers about herbal medicines. Then, Ray announced me as the next speaker. "Esther has worked with a cooperative in Cuernavaca, and she will tell you how this idea could help you here."

"In Cuernavaca, the women formed a cooperative. They make and embroider clothing and directly sell them at farmer's markets and festivals to earn a living," I told them. "They combine their products and take turns selling at the market. Everyone gets the full price they charged," I added, explaining,

"They cut out the middleman. Why pay a chunk of the profit to someone else to sell your goods?"

"The women used to live on near-starvation wages, but with this clothing cooperative organization, they are now earning enough to live in comfort."

These groups had the same interests I do since grassroots activism has been my life. The struggle for social justice and solidarity with people in other parts of the world like Mexico and Central America is my struggle too.

After our presentation, we stayed for lunch and sat around an open fire watching the women cooking enough food for the entire village. They arranged the tables in a field about forty feet by thirty feet, underneath a thatched roof. The area was open on both sides and was about fifty yards from the lake. Without fences, horses ran free, and dogs played in the water. We sat down to eat fish from the lake with homemade tortillas. I was impressed by how the indigenous people lived off the land; it was just second nature to them, while in larger Mexican cities, people depended on grocery stores or farmer's markets.

On the way home, we stopped in Taxco, a little southwest of Cuernavaca, and best known for its silver mine. "Taxco reminds me of photographs I've seen of Mediterranean villages, like in Greece," I said to Ray.

"It is quite the tourist spot and internationally known," Ray said. "People from around the world visit here."

White houses with red-tiled roofs dotted the mountainside, and cobblestone streets ran through many of the hamlets. In Taxco, we took a steep winding road up about five thousand feet to a fancy restaurant overlooking the city, where many American tourists dine. I thought it might be expensive, but we ate shredded beef simmered in a delicious sauce with rice and beans for five dollars each. We ate our meal overlooking the city. What a long and exhausting but inspiring day. Now I was ready for a good night's sleep.

When we arrived home, Ray carried me into the house. Sylvia and Louisa helped settle me in bed.

The support I received from Ray and my Mexican family here was so life-affirming. Coming here to Mexico was the best decision I'd ever made.

11

A Meaningful Meeting

RAY PICKED ME up this morning, and we went to a talk by a group of young Mexicans who had just returned from Nicaragua. A few of the guys carried me in my wheelchair up the stairs to the auditorium at CCIDD. Canadian religious groups, local priests, and a few citizens of Cuernavaca filled the room. I listened to the group speaking Spanish and noticed I had no problem understanding them, so I was acclimating well to this culture. All the members were in high spirits and eager to share their experiences.

"I thought the coffee trees would be tall, and I would need to stretch up to pick the coffee berries," a young man dressed in shorts and a light shirt said. "But the trees were about three feet high, and we sat on the ground with our legs stretched out and plucked them from the trees.

"We brought along yellow rain slickers because we knew it would be the rainy season. The slickers fascinated the Nicaraguans since the coats were not available in their country," he added. "They just picked coffee in their clothes, got wet, and lived with it."

"The people in the coffee-picking community were eager to communicate with us; they wanted to talk most of the night," the leader said. "We had to tell them that we needed to get sleep so we could work tomorrow."

"The Nicaraguans enjoyed having us come and visit, like anyone who is living a hard life and struggling," a woman with a backpack remarked. "It shows solidarity when people who live in other countries visit. Without the resources, the Nicaraguans can't leave," she said. "It is inspirational when others come to share in the poverty, in the food, and in the struggle and do whatever they can to help, if only for a short while."

She removed pamphlets from her backpack and passed them out to the audience. "You can read about ways that you can serve the people. Every bit helps. Despite Mexico not having a Contra War, the Nicaraguans were surprised that there were still poor people in Mexico," she said. "The government of Mexico is not as revolutionary as the Nicaraguans are led to believe."

"People here don't think poverty exists in the United States either, but some Americans don't have enough to eat and are homeless," I said. "Some are lucky enough to find a park bench or cardboard box to sleep on at night in the warmer months or in the Southern States."

This shocked the young Mexicans.

"Many Nicaraguan children eat only tortillas, rice, and beans for every meal; this concerned us," another member said. "After only three days of this diet, some of us got diarrhea. We needed fruits and other nutritious food, and so did the children."

Ray asked, "Why did you go to Nicaragua? And how did the experience affect you?"

"Many of us learned of the brutal Somoza years," the leader said. "We wanted to see how the Sandinista regime had changed Nicaragua."

"We saw a society where everyone takes part in decision making," another member said. "The government channels the resources of the countryside for human needs, not for the greed of corporations and capitalism."

"The Sandinista regime encouraged everyone to work together toward a better life," the leader said.

"Even though life is severe, the Nicaraguans know why it is so hard," I said. "The people understand because the media educates the people about why so many problems exist."

"This society was like a dream, where I could take part as a Christian, a socialist, and even as a communist for a moment in history," the leader remarked. "We tire of the struggle in Mexico. We lose inspiration. And now we realize the dream is a possibility because we saw it happen in Nicaragua. We were there to experience it. This reinforces our ideas and hopes and helps us believe in the possibility."

"I saw my egotism and realized that I have been self-centered, and now I want to be more helpful to others," a young woman said. "I observed how the Nicaraguan government helped disabled persons by building wheelchairs and selling them for less than $100 to those who need them. The cost to manufacture each one was $400. When I was in Nicaragua, I watched them being made," she added. "The Sandinista government moved the repair workshop to the hospital and repair bicycles to support the disabled and war-injured citizens."

"This is just part of society to serve others," another member said. "We must do more to help here in Mexico."

"The rigors of poverty forged people to work together," the leader said. "There is no such thing as a comfortable revolution."

"Nicaraguans love all kinds of Mexican and American music. They have such little to bring joy in life," the young lady said, adding, "It's hard work to get up every day to another problem like a hurricane. Nicaragua is an example of collaboration, rather than attacking each other and being divided."

I felt such an aura of warmth, a spiritual force, moving among us at the meeting. I'm sure people who have visited Nicaragua could identify much of what those who had just visited the country shared with us. These young people's eyes shone so brightly. They were so full of life, so idealistic, and yet they realized the work to improve Nicaragua was difficult. They had touched this painful, rebirth of a nation.

Who knows whether or not it will succeed? But it exists now and at least will continue to live in the memories of all the people who visited. The Nicaraguans have no choice; they cannot deny consciousness or the truth. They cannot cover up the light once it has broken through into the people's awareness and penetrated their hearts.

12

Nicaragua or Bust

THIS BRIGADE TALK confirmed my imagination of Nicaragua. It is difficult, not a utopia, and everyone needs to pull his or her weight. I must go there now while I am still able. To visit Nicaragua had been my dream for years, but I realized I was allowing my disability to stop me. What use could I be? Finding I have a terminal, disabling disease was life-changing. A person of my age could live for twenty years from the onset of ALS. Every year, I would lose more function, but gradually, so it would be difficult to notice at first.

When I finally realized that I would die of this disease, I asked myself, What do I want to do while there still is some time left?

That's when I decided I would apply my mind to go to Nicaragua. I'd worked with Wisconsin Coordinating Council on Nicaragua when I was less disabled.

In March 1985, I wrote in my journal, "I will visit Nicaragua, and if the door opens, fine." But by the start of 1987, I still hadn't made a connection.

Then, I met Sonia, who coordinates sister city projects from

Nicaragua. I felt akin to her, as she understood my wish to see Nicaragua, after having heard so much about the revolutionary process in that country.

When she called and said she found a school where I could live and improve my Spanish, I sent a letter to my family on August 5, 1987:

> Dear family,
>
> I remember ten years ago, on my thirty-sixth birthday, how committed my Iranian friends were during the Iranian Revolutionary War. In Berkeley, California, we joined many protests and educated ourselves to understand the United States' role. These experiences were significant events in my life. It opened me up to international activism, not just to issues in the local United States of America, but also to global issues. Going to Nicaragua is the climax of that commitment that started in Berkeley.
>
> Going to Nicaragua is scary because I am so secure and well cared for in Cuernavaca, Mexico. I'm not sure how much help I will find in Nicaragua. Putting my life in God's hands, I have faith I can be of some use. Maybe, I will stay for only a few months. It has

been my life's goal to go to Nicaragua;
I can't help myself.

I plan to write a journal, comparing
my hardships with the struggles in
Nicaragua. Nicaragua is giving me
the inspiration to move on, because
the Nicaraguan people do, despite
staggering odds. To stop struggling
would be to die, the same for me. I
want to keep going as long as I'm able,
God willing.

Please don't expect letters as often
because my hands are getting weaker,
and I need to save my writing energy
for my journal. Maybe we could phone
more.

Sonia will help me settle. I will send
my address when I arrive. I practice my
Spanish every day and am planning to
take a refresher class.

Love,
Esther

13

Meeting a Reporter

I ARRIVED IN Nicaragua the same week the US government munitions train ran over Brian Willson. He was sitting on the tracks protesting the arms headed for the Contras in Nicaragua when the train increased its speed. He continued to sit in civil disobedience. The train plowed into Brian, and he lost his legs; he now has artificial ones.

This brutality happens in other countries, where they hide the facts. In the States, the press should make it easier to bring the truth to light.

Wanting to show my support for Brian and the Nicaraguans, I attended the protest rally at the Managua embassy. I sat in the same circle in my wheelchair with the disabled Nicaraguans. I was so alive to be part of a group of people who wanted a change. Now I know; I am not alone.

I noticed a gentleman who was standing by me in the crowd staring at the book on my lap. The book, entitled Somoza and the Legacy of U.S. Involvement in Central America, by Bernard Diederich fascinated him. Why is he interested in this book? I thought. He walked from the shadows and said, "I noticed you are reading a book written in English, so I assume you speak the language."

"Yes," I said.

"My name is Jeremy," he replied. "I am a reporter who lives in California near the Naval Weapons Station in Concord," he said. "I was covering the scheduled protest, and I witnessed what happened to Brian."

"My name is Esther," I replied. "That must have been traumatic."

"Yes," Jeremy told me. "Brian gave a speech, saying each train that passes by here with munitions will kill people like you and me in Nicaragua. We must stop this train. Then the train sped up and plowed into Brian.

"Others on the tracks jumped free," Jeremy recalled. "Brian, because he was sitting on the tracks, could not. The train cut off his legs. His friends and his wife rushed to give first aid until the ambulance arrived. They saved his life.

"I came to Nicaragua to find out for myself and report what my country is doing down here," he added.

"Me too," I replied.

"In a wheelchair?" he asked.

"Yes. I was born in Switzerland, but now my family lives in the United States. What President Reagan and the US government are doing to this country appalls me. So I escaped."

Jeremy wanted to interview me and suggested we go out for dinner. He drove me to Sonia's home and said he would come to pick me up tonight around six o'clock. I was staying with Sonia until a high school outside Managua was available.

Jeremy arrived and helped me into the front seat of a Toyota he had rented. He stowed my wheelchair in the trunk. Since he reserved a table, the hostess immediately seated us. She had removed a chair for me, so I could wheel right up to the table.

The waiter brought the menus to the table and laid them on the white tablecloth in front of us. "Please order whatever you like," Jeremy said. "My newspaper gives me an allowance for meals, which includes people I interview."

"Thank you," I said to Jeremy. "I'll have the special with the seafood, deep-fried plantains, rice and beans, and a cabbage salad." I gave the waiter my order.

"And you, sir?" the waiter asked Jeremy.

"I'll have the same, except I would like the chicken."

"I think it worries Reagan that the Russians will take over in Nicaragua," Jeremy said. "We would then have another communist country, like Cuba, near the United States, and this one in Central America."

"My opinion is that Russia is present here to help Nicaragua, not control the country as the United States claims," I replied. "I've ridden in Russian Lada cars several times. There is a mixture of Japanese Toyota and Russian Lada cars here in Nicaragua. The reason that Russian vehicles are here is that they only cost $4,000 apiece—a simple basic economic fact of why Nicaraguans buy them.

"Russia is helping in other ways," I told him. "Every morning, I eat Russian wheat bread for breakfast. The other day I saw on TV that the Russian government shipped another boatload of grain here. Nicaraguans didn't have enough flour to make bread. Russia helped."

"But Nicaragua is also receiving Russian military equipment, rifles, and bullets," Jeremy said.

"Russia is the only country providing military hardware,"

I replied. "Nicaragua is like David in the Bible, defending itself against Goliath, the United States. The United States is supporting and supplying the Contras so they can attack Nicaraguans," I explained. "Nicaragua needs help!"

"Esther, I can see how strongly you feel about this," Jeremy said. "How can you ever return to the United States?"

"I am living in Mexico now and visiting here for a few months, with no plans to return to the United States."

The waiter brought our meals, and we stopped talking long enough to eat.

"I would like to hear more of your perspective on this conflict," Jeremy said. "I'd like to meet tomorrow for lunch?"

"Yes. I enjoy talking with you about how we view Nicaragua through our different lenses," I said.

Jeremy drove me to Sonia's house and helped me to the front door.

"I'll pick you up tomorrow around noon," he said. "How does that sound?"

"I'll see you then," I said as I settled into the closest chair.

Jeremy arrived the next day a few minutes before noon.

He walked and pushed me in my wheelchair to a quaint restaurant in a nearby park. After eating, we sat under some shade trees on a bench so we could talk in private.

"I would like to ask you a personal question," he said. "Tell me to mind my business if you don't want to answer," he added. "Why are you in a wheelchair?"

"A doctor diagnosed me as having the early stages of ALS, and I'm unsteady with my walker, so I have switched to a wheelchair."

"I'm sorry, Esther," Jeremy said. "I shouldn't have asked."

"No, it's fine, Jeremy. Since I have escaped the United States, I am doing better," I said. "I identify with the people of Nicaragua. With ALS, I struggle with the fact that my body is not doing what my mind and my spirit tell it to do," I explained. "The Nicaraguans hope for a better society, despite the handicap imposed by the US economic blockade and the underdevelopment of their country for many years. They will support their unity and self-determination, which is my constant struggle as well. I'm getting encouragement from being here—from seeing and experiencing their spirit, courage, and clarity of thinking."

"Besides the embargo, have you witnessed anything else?" he asked.

"Well, the misinformation campaign the United States is waging against Nicaragua isn't helping. Americans don't hear the true voice of Nicaragua because the United States media doesn't report it," I said. "While you are here, I hope you can discover the truth and enlighten citizens in the United States. Unless one seeks accurate information from people who've visited here and experienced it, one does not know what is happening or what people think of the revolution. When in the States, I often wondered what daily life was like down here. So even though my family didn't want me to visit Nicaragua, I put my faith in God and came to see and experience it for myself."

Jeremy drove me back to Sonia's house, and I told him I would move soon to a high school where I will improve my Spanish.

"Goodbye, Jeremy," I said. "I enjoyed spending time with you.

"I did too, Esther. I wish you well. I'll keep you in my prayers."

"Thank you, Jeremy."

I sat outside in my chair in the sunshine, waving as he drove away.

Glimpses of Culture

I'VE BEEN HERE in Nicaragua for two months. I now live in a high school outside of Managua, where I can improve my Spanish while being a part of the community. Speaking fluent Spanish is essential when I communicate with the Nicaraguans, and Jonathon, my teacher, helped me. I took classes twice a week and enjoyed seeing my progress.

Teenagers who attend the school here live in a poor barrio nearby. Students cannot buy any junk food at the school—no candy, soda, or potato chips. Little bags of peanuts, fruit, juices, and coconut bars made from locally grown products are available. The government is trying to promote these so the economy can survive. Consuming foods made in Nicaragua and not imported help.

Once in a while, some high school students come after school and give me a wheelchair ride. Sometimes they help me buy food at the local farmer's market. There I find delicious varieties of fruits and vegetables—limes, tangerines, and mandarin oranges are my particular favorites, but the papayas and guavas are also juicy and sweet. The lettuce, tomatoes, peppers, and jicama are crispy fresh for the salads I eat.

The first day the students took me to the market, I gave them about eighty cents, trying to encourage them to come back, and they didn't want to accept it.

"Then give it to your mother, please," I said as I handed it to Anika, the girl who came to see me the most.

"Thank you," she said and left.

The next day, Anika showed up at my door with a bunch of bananas. I got my purse out, ready to pay her.

"No. It is a gift from my mother," she said. "She would like to meet you. Could you visit us on Saturday? I'd arrive at one o'clock to give you a ride in your wheelchair; it's not far."

"I would enjoy visiting your family, Anika," I replied. "Thank you so much."

At seventeen years old, Anika is an attractive young lady. In the States, she would be considered a popular high school girl, maybe a cheerleader. She is interested in disco and rock music and would like to go to the National Music Festival in Managua, which includes folk music. But it is expensive even by my standards, so she won't be able to go. Lionel Richie and Michael Jackson are among her favorite singers.

On Saturday, Anika brought two of her older brothers— Juan, eighteen, and David, twenty-one. David already completed military service, and Anika's other brother is in the army right now. They helped carry me up into their home in the wheelchair.

"Mother, this is my friend, Esther. Esther, this is my mother, Ariana," Anika said, introducing me to her mother, a soft-spoken woman in her late forties. She spoke no English, but I could understand her fine. She figured out my Spanish with a little help from Anika.

"Your daughter is a great help when we go to the local farmer's market," I said. "She is a delightful young lady. I consider her, my friend."

"Gracias. I believe she is a good girl, too. And I have raised her to be helpful," Ariana said. "I wanted to meet you because Anika speaks so highly of you."

Anika blushed a little.

"I think you are special too, Anika," I said.

"Let us eat a little lunch together," Ariana said while showing us into the kitchen to a table and chairs.

As we entered, I smelled the pungent aromas coming from the stove. We had shredded chicken, which tasted like it had simmered in spices all morning long. Anika brought the pans to the table, along with a dish of homemade tortillas. We could garnish our tacos with chopped tomatoes, garlic, and sliced avocados. Anika led us in grace, and we all enjoyed sharing the meal. Fresh juicy tangerines, my favorite, were dessert.

"Muchas gracias. Esta comida es deliciosa," I replied with a smile.

"I am glad you like our food," Anika said.

After eating, we entered a modest living room with three decorations on the wall. The first was a woven picture of a fiesta, and the second, a painting of the Virgin Mary. On the same wall in the living room hung a portrait of Lenin. They saw no conflict with this.

Nicaraguans have had a social experience of repression, which many citizens in the United States have not experienced. They struggled for sheer existence during the Somoza years.

And now the Contras, backed by the United States of America, are ripping their country apart. I believe these people know what they believe. They see no conflict between their Christian faith and socialism. They believe in helping their neighbors, and they haven't seen the Soviet Union or Cuba forcing anything.

We sat talking for a while until it was time to leave. We said our goodbyes, and Anika's mother invited me to visit again. I thanked everyone for an enjoyable afternoon, and Juan and David carried me down the steps and back onto the street, where Anika pushed me home.

Tomorrow, I plan to go with a group to a fair to celebrate the countries that are helping Nicaragua, so I will need a good night's sleep.

15

Solidarity Fair with Witness for Peace

RAUL AND CARMEN came to pick me up in their Russian Lada car. Carmen helped me settle in the front seat, while Raul put my wheelchair in the back. Two members of the Solidarity Committee helped carry me in my wheelchair up the stairs when we arrived at the fair. A large sign showed the countries that helped and sympathized with Nicaragua. Printed in large red letters were East Germany, Switzerland, France, Canada, and the names of other Latin America countries.

I spent most of my time in the Swiss booth. I enjoyed talking with Gretchen, the young girl staffing the booth. She spoke with a Swiss-German dialect like my family did at our home. Gretchen could also speak English, so we went back and forth, speaking in both languages.

"The aid coming from our native country impresses me," she said. She pointed to a map of the sister cities in Switzerland. A small Swiss town neither of us had heard of donated over $30,000 to a sister village here in Nicaragua. "I learned the Swiss government has been supporting workers and technicians and paying their salaries ever since 1980," Gretchen said.

"A Swedish cooperative is remodeling the building at the Center for the Disabled in Managua where I work," I said. "They also donated several ultramodern wheelchairs to the center.

"At the high school where I lived, Canadians are helping to start a project so that the students can grow more of their food. Students are raising large gardens of tomatoes, beans, and corn.

"I enjoyed meeting you, Gretchen," I said. "Thank you for informing me about what my native land is doing to help Nicaragua."

Other countries had helped Nicaragua, so I moved on to other booths.

Holland had contributed a great amount of humanitarian aid and self-help projects. I learned about a Belgian brigade here helping to build a health clinic. These countries brought their workers because of the labor shortage caused by mobilizing so many Nicaraguans for the defense of the country. More women were working in jobs the men used to do, like during World War II in the States, symbolized by Rosie the Riveter.

Raul and Carmen met up with me as I exited the Canadian booth.

"We are ready to drive you home," they said.

"Thank you," I said. "I enjoyed my time here, learning how all the different countries were helping Nicaragua."

16

Letter Home

Dear family,

Note my new address on the envelope. I guess I should mention where I am living now. For the first few months, I was living at the high school outside Managua, where I took Spanish lessons from this great guy, Jonathon. I had little privacy, as I had to share the bathroom with the teachers because I was living in the school's office.

Now I am living in central Managua. The house is a Nicaraguan upper-middle class. I have my bedroom and a private bath. The shower rates a 10, which is in sharp contrast to the trickle I got at other places I lived. I can use my wheelchair throughout the house. It is spacious, and the doorways are wide. I am trying to use the walker more because I want to keep exercising.

I eat well compared to other people here. For breakfast, I eat two eggs, bread with real butter, and coffee; meat practically every day for lunch; and for supper, beans, rice, and milk. So I'm living in luxury, compared to the average Nicaraguan here, which makes me feel guilty. I pay $175/month for rent, which is a lot of money here.

Workers don't make a lot of money in Nicaragua. The problem of unemployment doesn't exist. Regardless of the low wages, Nicaraguans will work. A cleaning lady maybe makes $15/month, and schoolteachers earn $30/month.

I'm not sure how the economy works here in Nicaragua. Others tell me the government loans money with fair terms so people can buy houses and cars.

I even heard from some friends of mine that the Soviets loan money interest-free. In saying that, even having grown up in a capitalistic society, I am not suspicious of the Soviet Bloc. How can anyone be so altruistic as to give interest-free loans? They must attach strings. In the United States, I heard this slogan, "There is no such thing as a 'free lunch,'" yet in Nicaragua at the high school where I lived, they had a free lunch for the students, teachers, and myself—government-subsidized, and it often included meat.

I enjoy seeing a news broadcast about what the Soviets, Chinese, and Americans are doing, not only the United States as if it were the entire world. Watching the news with an equal time given to each country, I am informed about the world. I read in the newspaper today that the Soviet and Western countries contributed thousands of dollars so the Nicaraguan children could have a Merry Christmas. I wondered why Nicaragua doesn't make its own toys. Why don't they spend that money on a factory to create toys? And then I remembered the labor shortage.

Too many citizens are fighting against the Contras. The United States is supporting and supplying the Contras. I'm not sure I can ever live in the United States again.

Love you all,
Esther

17

Nicaragua in a Wheelchair

IN THE STATES, I attended support groups. But being disabled was all we had in common. My political views were another handicap; I wasn't able to express that part of myself. While in Nicaragua, I could discuss my political opinions because many people had the same views. I coped better with my physical disabilities, not being politically handicapped.

"Would I be able to work with the disabled? I identify most with them," I asked Sonia.

"There is a family who lives near a center called the Organization of Disabled Revolutionaries" (ORD). "I'll discuss it with them."

I became a volunteer at the center after Sonia's friends said they had an extra room. They would give me a chance to practice my Spanish, and I would teach them English. Living two blocks away from the center, I traveled to work by taxi. I volunteered to do rudimentary translating, but mostly I met with the disabled of Nicaragua, helping in any way I could.

Oh, how young these disabled people were. My disability had begun at thirty-eight, and by now—at forty-four—I'd been in my chair for only six months. In my youth, I was active, with no physical restrictions. Almost everyone in Nicaragua in a wheelchair was under thirty—victims of the war, accidents, and preventable diseases like polio. The Somoza regime did not vaccinate its people. But immediately after the Revolution, Sandinistas vaccinated children against polio. That was why one didn't see crippled children under the age of eight. The Sandinistas believed it was both a financial and a humanitarian decision.

In Nicaragua, wheelchairs were a means of transportation. People traveled five or six kilometers from their homes to work or school. They tilted their chairs back and wheeled themselves up and down off the curbs. I couldn't do that with mine, so I wasn't sure how they did it.

The Nicaraguan wheelchairs impressed me. Factories made them in Nicaragua, but the demand far outstripped the supply. Although the United States produced wheelchairs used in Nicaragua, because of the US economic blockade, the spare parts to repair them were difficult to find. This embargo caused tremendous hardships for the Nicaraguan people. One of my jobs at the ORD center was to find repair parts for these US chairs.

My wheelchair was the Rolls 2000, touted to be the latest model in sports chairs in the States. When I first arrived in Nicaragua, I thought my chair would be the envy of everyone. Surprise, the Nicaraguans could maneuver better in theirs than I could in mine.

Nicaraguans had access to the Ralf Hotchkiss Appropriate Technology wheelchair. Ralf, an engineer from Berkeley, California, had a bicycle accident that rendered him a paraplegic while still in high school. Because the wheelchairs available for purchase didn't satisfy his needs, he designed his own wheelchair. He attended an engineering college in California.

He believed that supplying a wheelchair to all who needed it would lead to the independence of those who couldn't walk and a better chance to integrate into society. Five years ago, he came to Nicaragua to show the manufacturers how to make better chairs.

The disabled, along with myself, attended the First National Special Games for the Nicaraguan War and Civilian Disabled held in mid-November 1987. In my wildest dreams, I never imagined riding on an army truck in my wheelchair. The Sandinista soldiers placed long wooden boards used as a ramp so they could push the chairs up into the truck. It thrilled me to ride on the back of a military vehicle winding through the streets of Managua with a police escort. More than six hundred people came, spending Thursday, Friday, and Saturday night at the military school in Managua. The soldiers of the Sandinista Popular Army helped us over a curb or to travel up a hill in our wheelchairs if we needed it.

We continued to the military school for lunch; they pulled the chairs from under the tables so that our wheelchairs would fit under them. A Sandinista soldier was feeding a young man about thirty years old, patiently waiting until he swallowed before offering him the next spoonful. The man had no hands; in their place, metal hooks opened and closed to help him pick up things. The soldier showed such gentleness and caring; it touched me.

After thanking the Sandinista soldier for his help, I started a conversation. "Hi, my name is Esther," I said.

"Mine is Emmanuel, I've seen you around the ORD center."

"I'm glad to meet you," I said.

We talked, and when comfortable, I asked what had happened to him.

"During the revolution, I had a homemade bomb and wanted to throw it at some Contras who were causing trouble and camping right outside our village," Emmanuel explained. "But, it exploded and blew my hands away."

Unsure of what to say, I touched his shoulder. "I'm sorry that happened to you," I said.

"Thank you for caring, Esther," he said. He gave me such a sweet smile.

"How did you escape the Contras? Didn't they try to find you?" I asked.

"I jumped into a latrine they had just built and stayed quiet, biting my lips because the pain was unbearable. "They left after searching the bushes. I stumbled home. My mother sent for the village doctor, and he bandaged up what I had left of my hands. I've had several operations and was fitted with this device so I can pick up things, but I haven't mastered it yet. Even with all that has happened, I am proud I stood up for my country."

"You are brave, Emmanuel. I am so sorry that my country is supporting the Contras. Many Americans do not know what their government is doing," I said. "I came here for the truth and to send it back to the United States."

The soldiers formed us into lines as we began the march from the military school to the Plaza of the Revolution in Managua. The Sandinista soldiers pushed us to the plaza.

At the ceremony, Emmanuel and I sat next to each other. We sang the national anthem of Nicaragua, "Salve a ti Nicaragua"

(Hail to Nicaragua). We faced the sunset through the trees in the park. The red and black Sandinista flag waved gently in the breeze. The sun was a brilliant orange-yellow globe as it sank below the horizon in the darkening blue sky. Tears rolled down my cheeks. I felt such a connection to these Nicaraguans who had fought so hard to save their country. These people gave me hope to go forward and to face my struggles as my disease progresses.

The next morning, the First National Wheelchair Basketball Games took place in a local park. These disabled people played rough, and once in a while, a participant fell out of a chair after crashing into someone else. Within seconds, soldiers helped whoever fell back into their wheelchair, and the game continued. Although disabled, the players could take part in a basketball tournament. We were making progress.

These Sandinista soldiers defended us from the Contras taking over the country. I often pictured Nicaragua as an example to the world where people are working together to make a new way of living—coming out of the old, oppressive life under Somoza. Out of the destructive dictatorship came a new light, a promised land to share. There was hope for Nicaragua.

The next day after breakfast, we traveled to Jiloa, a volcanic crater lake about twenty kilometers outside Managua, surrounded by hills. Here the disabled paraplegics competed in swimming contests. Teresa, a friend of mine, swam with the men in these games. She dragged her legs behind her and used her strong upper body to swim through the water. She didn't win but was proud of taking part. I think she swam in her slip and a shirt. Many people swam with shorts and just let them dry on their bodies.

I wanted to put my feet in the water, so the soldiers pushed me close to the edge. But I couldn't roll in farther because the races continued and I didn't want to get in the way. If the wheelchair got wet, the salt in the water could corrode the bearings, so I didn't get too close. Afterward, I crawled into the lake to experience the cool waves washing over me. The water tasted a little like sulfur as the gases bubbled up from the bottom of the volcano, but it wasn't overpowering.

The water looked clear, not polluted, with clean sand on the beach. Near the shore, a thin old man with white hair looked out at the swimmers. He said he was from Istiling. He looked like a white person, a gringo. I knew of German settlements in that area.

"I got my wheelchair this week," he said.

"When I first got mine, I felt a little lost," I explained. "But after a month, I was doing fine."

He continued talking, and he had a pleasant, outgoing personality. We were both happy to communicate, not isolated, but part of something. With a glint in his eyes and a shy manner, he asked if I had a cigarette.

"I don't, but I would like one too," I replied.

"I need one, but none of the stores around here are open," he said.

"Let's watch. Maybe we can get one from someone who is smoking," I answered.

A soldier who smiled at us came by, and I noticed a pack in his shirt pocket, so I asked, "Please, do you have a cigarette?"

"I have one left," he said.

"Oh, then don't bother. I don't want to take your last one," I said.

The Sandinista soldier insisted on giving the cigarette to us. I thanked him for his generosity. The old man and I shared the cigarette, exchanging puffs and discussing our lives.

A police escort again accompanied us as we left for home. The traffic stopped because the road wasn't wide enough for twenty military trucks in a row to pass. The soldiers wheeled us into the army truck, and I realized I could not take any more sun. Domingo, one of the Sandinista soldiers, offered me a towel to cover my head and arms, so I stayed. My arms got sunburned and turned deep red with blisters. It has been a year, and I still have brown blotches above my wrists, a reminder of that day on the army truck going back to Managua in the scorching bright tropical sun.

I would have loved to spend another night, as the soldiers had planned a rifle-shooting contest, but I knew I was overdoing it. Exhausted and sunburned, I asked if someone could give me a ride home, which someone did after the sun went down.

The first thing when I got home, I asked an employee if she would please make me a piña, a fresh pineapple.

"That is delicious. Thank you," I said.

I loved the Nicaraguan white pineapple, with its white meat inside and more tart than those in the States.

At eight o'clock, I watched the news; there was coverage of the games which I enjoyed.

The next day, I slept all day. Then I showered, changed clothes, got cleaned up, and rested. I watched the news that night and enjoyed the coverage of the rifle-shooting contest. I wished I had the stamina to go, but I didn't.

18

Returning to My Mexican Family

NICARAGUA WAS INCREDIBLY moving. The country, the people, the government, the news media, and the Catholic Church—all were sane. Yes, shelves were half-empty, or half-full depending on your view. People didn't have much food, but they had enough to prevent starvation. With the US dollars I had, I ate well. I felt guilty knowing I ate better than most people in Nicaragua.

The Nicaraguan revolution was an honest process. There was no battering of society and no gross contradictions. The lies told by the Empire to the North did not penetrate the psyche of the people. The spirit of the people was clean, like crystal clear water.

Yes, the people of Nicaragua suffered, but they did so with clarity. Nicaragua was a humbling experience; the Nicaraguan struggle was as hard as mine. The handicaps and emotional pain were not individualistic but a collective experience. Everyone suffered. My being there with my disability was no big deal to any Nicaraguan. Many people lived in Nicaragua with disabilities and wheelchairs. None of them got a check for $280 a month like I did. They earned around $20 a month or less. They couldn't fly out of their condition in an airplane like I could, although my disease flew with me. They possessed solidarity, which I envied.

I was going back to Cuernavaca. I needed more help than I was getting here. The worst thing was that no one thought of me as having special needs. Friends here said they would help, and then they didn't show up or even call to tell me why they couldn't. I become depressed and diverted my attention with thoughts of suicide.

While in Cuernavaca, Ray's attention had stopped those ideas. Lately, I'd had a flimsy support network. I needed solid support like Sylvia gave me. I had little energy left, and it was hard to serve others when you were weary of life yourself. The help didn't take me seriously. I felt like a "nonhuman," whose needs are always on the back burner—until shoved off the stove into a paralyzing depression. I found no balance between life's pains and joys.

The disabled here touched me deeply; I still would like to live with them. But I was homesick, and my health had deteriorated.

I flew back to Cuernavaca, Mexico, and arrived late in the evening. Sylvia and her youngest daughter, Juanita, picked me up at the airport. They ran down the aisle and gave me a big hug. I loved seeing their smiling faces.

"We missed you," they said in unison. "We are so glad to have you back with us."

"Me too," I answered.

I loved being back with my "Mexican family"—the way the children served me with smiles on their faces. If I asked for something, they responded within a reasonable amount of time. For a normal thing like a glass of water, I didn't have to wait ten minutes. No big deal; they brought it. I was treated like an adult here—an adult with dependency problems.

Sylvia and I understood each other. This understanding was reflected in the way she treated me, and how she helped take care of my needs conveyed her concern for others. The twinkle in her eyes when we were talking showed me how much she liked me. Even though she may be in a hurry, she took time to visit with me.

Today, Juanita squeezed me a glass of lemon juice, and I was reminded of how happy she was to help. She is such a delightful child.

Sylvia made special meals for my homecoming. The next morning, she made one of my favorite breakfasts. She cooked fluffy scrambled eggs mixed with cooked quinoa and creamy queso fresco. Then she piled it into warmed corn tortillas and topped it with crumbled chorizo.

For lunch, we ate a grilled chicken salad garnished with tangerine slices, toasted almonds, raisins, jicama, radishes, and avocado slices, along with fresh greens. Silvia made my favorite honey mustard salad dressing to drizzle on top. I hadn't eaten this well since leaving for Nicaragua.

"I made you an appointment to visit my naturista doctor tomorrow afternoon," Sylvia said. "If you don't want to go, I will call and cancel, but I am worried about you being in Nicaragua for four months."

I told her I would go.

"Thank you, Esther," Silvia said. "I'll feel better knowing you are fine.

"My older daughters won't eat this pineapple unless I cut it up for them," she added. She got out her knife and the board and cut down. The knife was dull.

I told her how, in Nicaragua, a man on a bicycle would go around from house to house to sharpen knives. He would sit on his bike with a flint stone attached to a wheel. Spinning the wheel, he would sharpen the knives.

"I have a sharpener right here in my home," Sylvia said.

She went to the stairway made of raw cement. With a few sweeps across the concrete, she sharpened the cutting edge of the knife. She came back and quickly cut up the pineapple.

I remembered we had an old sharpening stone about two feet wide at The Wooden Shoe, where I lived for three years. We would sit on a seat on the apparatus and pedal to make it spin—sharpening axes, knives, and gardening tools.

After lunch, I asked Juanita if she could take me to the park down the street.

"I'll be happy to," she said. "Mamá asked me to do some errands, and I'll come back later this afternoon. I'll meet you at Grandma's shop."

"Thank you so much," I replied. " I appreciate your help, sweetheart."

Juanita wheeled me down the hill to the park. I had the entire day to myself. It was a whole different world, like paradise, sitting out in the bright sunshine with the splendid trees- laurel, guava, palms, and other trees I didn't know. I had a particular affection for guava trees.

Last time here at the park, I could wheel myself up to the

guava trees, grab onto some lower branches, and pull myself up to stand. Today, a gardener had trimmed the trees that hung over the walk, which disappointed me. A guava tree grew right in front of the house in Nicaragua, where I lived, and the two neighbor girls liked to climb. It was their playground, and they would eat the green and hard guavas. Here we bought them from the store or market when they were yellow and soft; I much preferred them that way.

I must count my blessings. There wasn't another park as wonderful as this in the whole of Cuernavaca, and I could often visit, as it was so close to the house. Today, El Popo and, to El Popo's left, Iztaccihuatl, two volcanoes with their snowcaps, appeared in the distance. What a sight to behold! I felt I was back in Switzerland, looking at the Alps for a while. These two ancient volcanoes had been there from before the indigenous people. The natives had a legend about the sleeping woman in the Popo, just like the monk and the Jungfrau story in Switzerland. A monk was making sure that the Jungfrau is safe from any lecherous advances. In Popo, there was an Indian watching a sleeping woman, hoping she would wake up, just like the fairy tale about Sleeping Beauty.

Between the park and the volcanoes, I could view the people's yards and the patios of all the lovely homes. All around me were vegetation, flowers, and greenery.

I needed to go to the Xerox shop, so I rolled myself down the flat street, staying on the road because the sidewalks were unpredictable and narrow. A telephone pole created an obstacle because I couldn't maneuver around it. Cracks in the sidewalks made it hard to roll. Streets here were mainly for people, anyway. Everybody walked in or pushed their carts in the street, and the traffic slowed to accommodate the pedestrians.

I was in a barrio, a neighborhood. Many shops here were little rooms off the street with a door. The doorway to the bakery was only three feet wide. I couldn't get in with my wheelchair, but all the shopkeepers were friendly and would come out to find out what I wanted.

I had copies Xeroxed and bought a hazelnut chocolate bar and a little bouquet to brighten my room. At the copy store, on the wall, hung a poster of the Golden Gate Bridge. I imagined a picture of the two Mexican volcanoes in a travel agent's office in Berkley, California, where my sister Regina lived. My mind went from Berkeley and then to Mexico in the blink of an eye; I enjoyed the views.

I stopped at Grandmother's shop to say hi and chatted for a while. "When I was growing up, this area was very different," she said. "The streets here in Cuernavaca were all dirt, all the houses were smaller, and horses pulled carts in the street."

It was late afternoon before Juanita showed up to roll me home.

"Goodbye," I said. "I'll see you at home."

"If God wills it," she murmured.

Images flashed through my mind of what an earthquake would do in just a matter of seconds. Mexico City experienced an 8.0 magnitude earthquake on September 19, 1985. The event caused about $3 billion to $4 billion in damage and killed at least five thousand people, so I understood that "God willing" was a common phrase, especially among the elderly.

I remembered a quake in Nicaragua, where I'd felt like I was on an ocean liner when we hit a massive wave, or maybe a whale. I remained on my bed when the shaking began. My books fell off the shelf, and a glass trinket shattered on the floor. I believe that one registered 5.6. For a month or more, I felt insecure. When using my walker, I often worried that I might fall, but it was disconcerting to know that the earth could move under me as well. In this part of the world, earthquakes were frequent, and the people believed "God willing" was their reality.

19

Going to a Naturista Doctor

IN THE MORNING after breakfast, Sylvia helped me find a taxicab, and the driver let us off on a one-way street. She pushed me the rest of the way to the small house that was an office, squeezed between two large buildings. A flagstone walkway on the green grass and two small steps made it harder to push the wheelchair. There was always someone willing to help. The doctor carried me into the office in his arms and set me gently back in my chair, which Sylvia brought into the building.

There was a little natural food store in the front, with some books, and I purchased one about a garlic, onion, and lemon cure.

After about a half an hour wait, the doctor invited me into his office. I liked him right away; he was a big man with somewhat of a belly. He had a kind face with a subtle glint in his eye.

Dr. Rodrigues said he spoke no English. I thought He speaks some English. But I understood what he meant; he would like to keep the conversation in Spanish. Sylvia told me he left the country periodically and had practiced in Cuernavaca for at least eight years. Sylvia saw him eight years ago when he first prescribed a diet and several teas to help her with nerve problems, depression, and fatigue when she couldn't even leave the house. Now she was an active woman selling Tupperware.

The doctor and I talked alone at first. I told him in Spanish how my problems started in 1980, and that, by 1987, Lou Gehrig's disease was my diagnosis. When I arrived in Cuernavaca, I was taking amphetamines to wake up in the morning, antidepressants during the day, and Valium so I could sleep at night. Now I only took Valium once in a while, but I drank coffee every morning. Sylvia said he would tell me to stop doing that, but he didn't.

"Since you only drink coffee once a day and are addicted to it, try to taper off," he said. "When you don't need it anymore, quit."

I guess he realized I had been through a lot of drugs; some coffee wouldn't make much difference.

He prescribed a natural diet, as Sylvia had told me he would, of fruit in the morning and raw oats or some other whole-grain cereal with honey or whole-grain bread with ricotta cheese. In the morning, I should drink a variety of teas. Lunch should be a raw salad of grated carrots, beets, onions, celery, and garlic with white meat like chicken grilled in lemon juice and salt or fish, along with soup or a macaroni product made of soy called sopa. A toasted tortilla with cheese and salsa was also fine. For supper, I could repeat breakfast. As a snack between meals, Dr. Rodrigues recommended an apple or an orange and the juice of one lemon or one orange a half hour before I ate.

The most intriguing thing he said was, "You need to buy nettle leaves, called Ortega or Mala Madre leaves."

I knew what he was talking about when he opened an impressive medical book on herbs. There was a full-page drawing of this plant, and I recognized the stinging nettle, which we ate when it was a young shoot in the spring at The Wooden Shoe in New Hampshire. The nettles grew around old barns, even in Wisconsin. We would pick them and cut them up, wearing gloves because they sting, having a similar substance to that found in bee venom. That was why it was called the stinging nettle.

"People with arthritis or rheumatism find it helpful too. Use the whole plant, not just the leaf; it needs to be fresh. It can't be dry," he explained. "Lash your skin on the areas affected, which would be on your arms, on your legs, and on your spinal column up to the back of your head. This process will stimulate your circulation and get things moving."

"I am so much better in Cuernavaca. My disease is almost arrested when I'm living here. Not having to cope with a change in climate is so important. Every day the weather is the same," I remarked. "Before I got sick, it would have bored me to tears, but now I appreciate it. In Wisconsin, I experienced all the changes, from the hottest weather in August to the brief autumn. And then the winter comes fast and furious, bringing with it snow and ice. Winter means cocooning myself in the house to stay warm and prevent falling. Sometimes I believe I would rather live here disabled than live in the United States without my disease. I don't enjoy being disabled, but I have had that thought."

Looking around his office, I noticed books covering many medical studies, including Chinese medicine. A colored chart on the wall depicting the chakras of the human body interested me. He struck me as a man interested in healing and always open and ready to hear the latest and newest things. He would learn from all the different disciplines and sciences to find what worked best for his patients.

I imagined that, as I went on with the treatment, I would gain a lot of confidence in him. I would see him again because he was not robbing me; it cost me twenty thousand pesos (less than ten dollars) for a consultation. The doctor prescribed nine different teas; each bag of dried leaves made twenty cups of tea and cost a thousand pesos (fifty cents).

My new doctor was an innovative healer, interested in the art of medical science. I knew that, if I did my part, he would do his, and we could work in a partnership.

"If you drink one soda or eat one slice of white bread, you will set your health back two days," he warned me. "You must stick to the diet and not cheat. Please, start the diet tomorrow."

Stephen Hawking also had Lou Gehrig's disease, and he published a book about his theories on the cosmos. He proved that people with ALS could continue on their life's path and do great things. We shouldn't give up. We must live our lives to the fullest. Stephen's work gave me hope.

The universe goes on forever, death is not final, and there is something after death. Life on earth is so brief compared to eternity. Who knows what happens afterward?

I knew that the prescribed diet and the lashing with the stinging nettle would not cure me of my illness, but it might help me feel better.

My entire Mexican family celebrated with me this evening. Sylvia made a shrimp casserole with scallions, garlic, and chili peppers poured over corn tortillas and queso fresco crumbled on top. We also had Mexican rice browned in oil, cooked, and blended with fresh boiled tomatoes, garlic, and onions, topped with cilantro. Juanita even made cherry empanadas for dessert.

"Tonight, we celebrate you being back with us," Sylvia said. "Tomorrow, you start your new diet."

20

Visiting the Guild House

TODAY, I NEED to take an adventure by myself. I took a cab to the Guild House, a five-minute drive away in an upper-class neighborhood where the houses are walled. A caretaker keeps the Guild House grounds neat with shady trees and splashes of colorful flower beds bordering the lawn. An English woman manages a little shop and a library within the building. "Could someone help me up these two stairs, please?" I asked. "It looks sunny on the second floor."

"Wait a minute," she replied. "I'll find someone to help."

Time passed, and I wondered if anyone was coming when the gardener and another man walked into the library. They lifted me in the wheelchair up the two steps to a delightful elevated room with light streaming in the tall ceiling-to-floor windows, filling the entire room. I smiled and thanked them.

The stacked books with their colorful bindings invited me to choose one to read. A tiny black book brought back memories of reading it in college. Although it was in Spanish,

I could read it. Thank you, Jonathon. After browsing other books, I asked for help again. The same gentlemen carried me to the first floor. I took El Profeta (The Prophet) by Khalil Gibran, and I checked out the book, giving my address to the librarian, and rolled me out the 1st-floor door and into the bright sunny day.

Rolling myself around the block, I saw a casa for sale; it was the only one without walls. There was a hedge, a swimming pool, a large house with tall trees, and a drive with the little gardener's cottage at the end.

"This property is for sale at $650,000," a realtor who'd approached me said. "Would you like to see the house?"

"No, thank you. But the house is charming," I said.

Another employee was leaving for lunch, and I asked him to please bring me a taxi.

This was a bonus—meeting people who had time to talk. The caretaker, the gardener, the cook's helper, and the employees of these vast mansions made me welcomed.

"The owners only come here on the weekends because they work in Mexico City all week," the gardener said. "We are the people who are enjoying the homes most since we live in them all week long. The owners don't know each other, but the employees do."

The workers were from impoverished barrios, where they had a sense of community. People talked and knew each other, while the owners drove up on the weekends and stayed within their walls.

I wondered what happened to these employees as they aged, so I asked, "Do your employers give you retirement benefits?"

"No, but we save what we can, and our families care for us as we age; this is an important part of our culture."

As my taxi drove up, I smiled.

"Thank you for a delightful afternoon, and I wish you all well," I said.

21

Celebration Differences

I WOULD CELEBRATE a part of the Christmas season with my friend, Mea; her husband, Don Pedro; and my adorable godchild, Maria de La Paz. They lived in Emiliano Zapata, a little southeast of Cuernavaca. I was interested in how Mexico celebrated the Christmas season, so I researched.

The Christmas celebration in Mexico was longer than that in the United States, starting on December 16 and ending on January 6. There was a series of parties and processions to represent Mary's and Joseph's search for a manger before the birth of Jesus. Residents cut intricate designs in paper bags and placed a candle inside each to light the way up the steps to their doors.

A procession headed out after dark from a local church. A selected girl and boy played the parts of Mary and Joseph going to houses to find a place to stay. Some people rejected them, but when they were accepted, the nativity scene received carved images of Mary and Joseph, and the children said a prayer of thanks. Often they sat down to a meal together. Spanish evangelists started this tradition to teach indigenous people about the Christmas story.

Another tradition used a seven-starred piñata made of clay or paper-mâché filled with candy or small gifts and suspended from the ceiling. The blindfolded children took turns swinging at the piñata with a stick; often, parents moved the piñata up and down to make the game more difficult. When the piñata broke, the children scrambled for the spilled treasure. This secular tradition of fun and games for the children harkened back to the Spanish evangelists who wanted to teach Christianity. A piñata represented the devil, who attracted people with the goods of the world. The seven-point star showed the seven cardinal sins. The Christian faith, which defeated evil and released the bounty for humankind, was the stick.

On Christmas Eve, Mexican families went to midnight Mass and returned home to a late dinner. They didn't exchange gifts then. On January 6, Dia de Los Reyes (the Day of the Kings), they celebrate the three wise men traveling to bring their gifts to baby Jesus. The children waited all year for their gifts, which symbolized the gold, frankincense, and myrrh given to Jesus. With the cultural influence of the United States, Santa Claus came to some Mexican homes.

While I was in Nicaragua, the natives celebrated the immaculate conception of the Virgin Mary Purisima on December 8. They placed a statue of the Virgin Mary in the corner of a family's house on a decorated altar. Around it, the family arranged chairs for the invited relatives, friends, and neighbors to celebrate Purisima.

Once all the guests arrived, they chanted a question, "Quién causa tanta alegría" (Who causes so much happiness)?

The family who lived in the home chanted their reply, "La Concepcion de Maria."

Whistles, tambourines, and other musical instruments intermixed with prayers to the virgin. Everyone then shared fruits, traditional sweets, and caramels.

Children went to a different house every evening for a week. They sang for the family and, in return, received a little treat. When I was in Nicaragua, we gave out sweet lemons, prized for their mild flavor, somewhat like watered-down lemonade. The lady across the street gave away little bags of sugar, maybe about half a cup. Considering Nicaragua had shortages, the children felt it was a real treat.

The giving away of sugar reminded me of when I was living in an upper-middle-class neighborhood, three blocks from the Hotel Intercontinental in Managua, Nicaragua. After spending a month in a poor barrio of the Sierra Mesta, on the outskirts of Managua at a school, I moved there. Near the holidays, children came to the door to beg. The owners of the house left for a vacation in Las Vegas, and employees answered the door saying, "We have nothing here; we are poor too. We have no bread."

We had bread in the kitchen.

One of the two little girls asked if we could spare a spoon of sugar instead. The employees gave her nothing, sending both children away empty-handed. I still remembered the scene; I was too slow to respond. Otherwise, I would have given them money to buy bread.

The next day, an old woman came to our house, and I quickly said, "Yes, I will give you something. It's Christmas." I gave her enough to buy food. It wasn't much, but it made me feel good to help her and let her know someone cared.

22

Christmas in Emiliano Zapata

I WAS SPENDING Christmas with the La Paz family. Outside, on the street, I saw the Campesinos go by on their horses as they traveled to their fields. As they crossed the bridge over the river, a young man and a lad were riding on the same horse. Through the open window, I heard the echo of the soothing clip-clop on the cobblestone streets.

This evening, I watched about a hundred children coming down the hillside carrying candles walking in a parade. Some of them were barefoot. The group marched down the street, singing their songs and going to the homes of the residents in the village. The house next door gave them oranges and goodies, and we offered a bag of cookies and peanuts that Mea and her daughter had prepared. The celebration reminded me of Halloween in the States.

On the night of Christmas Eve, the children carried maypoles with pink and white streamers and flowers on top, and the girls wore white dresses and crowns made of pink and white crepe paper roses. They wandered all around Emiliano Zapata from 8:00 p.m. until midnight. One young girl riding on a burro represented Mary, while her Joseph led her around.

Adults and children willingly took turns pushing my wheelchair. We walked through the village with the burro leading the way through the rocky streets and the dusty dirt roads, and me and my wheelchair along for the ride. What a gift! I thought. Except for the electric lighting, the time could have been two thousand years ago in Bethlehem, and we were all traveling to the stable to worship baby Jesus.

The procession led us to the main cathedral, where there was a program complete with shepherds dressed in their mantles. A "devil" tried to tempt or distract one shepherd from completing his mission to visit the infant Jesus in Bethlehem by offering him wine, and he became drunk. A second shepherd was handed tacos and food, and he gobbled up all the food. The last one received a hundred cards that he could mail to his friends to show how important he was. Instead of visiting Jesus, they all took part in each temptation given them. Then the angel came and chastised them, saying Christmas was not about the trappings, but the birth of Jesus.

When we got home around 1:00 p.m., the family sat down to a bowl of pozole made with pork and chicken and seasoned with chilies, garlic, and oregano. Maria and her mother had made the soup earlier in the day. A salad made of shredded lettuce and sliced radishes with lime wedges on the side was a refreshing addition.

We all went to bed, satisfied, and ready for a long night's sleep.

In the morning, I awoke to a heavenly smell coming from the kitchen.

"What smells so good?" I called out to Mea.

"I'm making empanadas for breakfast; everyone will be up soon."

Maria, with a friendly smile, bounded into my room, jumped into bed with me and hugged me. "Feliz Navidad, Madrina" (Merry Christmas, Godmother), she said.

She meant everything, this godchild of mine. She had been such an antidepressant ever since I'd met her. She pushed me in my wheelchair around the house, and when Don Pedro got up, we all gathered in the kitchen for breakfast. Afterward, we all settled into the living room, where he plugged in the lights on the tree, while we prepared to open presents.

I bought gifts for the family. A fruitcake for Don Pedro—I remembered how much he liked the Basler Läckerli my mother sent them last year. Just like fruitcake, those Swiss Christmas bars are full of candied fruits like orange and lemon peel and cinnamon. "Gracias, Esther," he said. He smiled at me and began slicing the cake for all of us to enjoy. He reminded me so much of my father, who also enjoyed fruitcake and Basler Läckerli during the holidays. Daddy had a darker complexion, too, being of Italian Swiss heritage.

I gave Mea a watch someone had given me, which I couldn't use, and a handkerchief with a Swiss design embroidered in Spanish, "Feliz Navidad."

"Thank you, Esther, maybe now I won't be late," she said.

We all chuckled.

Maria's gift was dear to my heart, just as she was. The minute I saw it in a specialty shop in Oaxaca, I knew it would be the perfect Christmas gift for her. Her favorite color was blue, and I found a white dress with ruffled tiers, tied at the waist with a blue ribbon. Blue hand-embroidered flowers at the neck and bottom edge of each layer decorated the front.

When she opened it, she held it up to herself and spun around laughing. "I'm a princess. Thank you so much, Madrina," she said. "It is the most beautiful dress I have ever seen."

I got a book on a lemon and garlic cure for helping the nerves from Don Pedro and a session with the local curandero from Mea. Maria gave me a little bouquet she'd picked from the garden. For her birthday, last year, I had sent her a kit for making potholders, and she made me one for Christmas.

"Gracias, little one," I said as I gave her a big hug.

"I'm not so little anymore," she replied.

She was right. Maria de La Paz, or Picke as she liked to be called, was only eleven years old and was taller than her mother, with long dark hair and expressive eyes. She had a sweet smile, with straight rows of pearly teeth, just like young kernels of baby corn.

"When will you lend me your blue eyes?" she often teased me.

"When you lend me your teeth of corn?" I would say to her.

We would both giggle and, I would tickle her to make her laugh out loud.

Picke was so affectionate. She would come to visit me in my room and ask me to brush her hair or rub her back; I liked to give affection too. She was like a younger sister or a daughter I never had. She was very intelligent and disciplined at doing her schoolwork and too much of a perfectionist at times.

She had done so much for me with her uplifting personality. She was easy to laugh, with a bright mind and a quick wit. Pické lightened my day as she dashed in and out of my room. It never annoyed me. She was the bright star in my universe, my special antidepressant. Now she was on vacation from school; I hoped she could be playful, like a child, again.

Today we were preparing a special dinner. There was a turkey roasting in the oven, and I would help Pické with making an Ensalada de Noche Buena. There were a lot of ingredients in this festive salad—lettuce, apples, carrots, oranges, pineapple, jicama, pecans, and pomegranate seeds. At Christmastime, people served this salad because it was so colorful. I washed all the ingredients in the sink, and Pické cut them into little pieces.

Mea was preparing the tamales made of cornmeal dumplings filled with queso fresco, and her husband was wrapping them in soaked corn husks and putting them to steam in a large-capacity double boiler.

When we finished making the meal, we gathered out on the patio and enjoyed this traditional meal.

Later in the afternoon, I was sitting and reading the lemon and garlic book I'd received from Don Pedro. Lemons, lettuce, almonds, and, above all, olive oil were helpful for the nervous system. My stomach seemed to reject all other kinds of fats, but I liked olive oil. I guessed my intuition about what was healthy for me must be right. I knew it was nutritious and used in Spain, Italy, and Greece.

Pické, with her friendly smile, just came into the room, and my heart was full. She'd been such a beautiful addition to my life ever since I met her at the end of May 1987, when her mother, working at CCIDD, left flowers and a note saying she would like to get to know me. Ever since then, we'd been friends. Mea and Don Pedro had even asked me to be Maria's godmother.

Mea and Ray are my guardian angels, sent from God. So was Jan, who got me in touch with Ray. They had faith in the human spirit and believed a disabled person could still live a fulfilled life.

Disabled people need others to encourage them to do what they can do for themselves with help, but not do everything for them. Help may be financial, educational, or moral support. This is true in a family, in a community, or on a national or an international level. OXFAM (Oxford Committee for Famine Relief) is an example of a charity that does this well. The OXFAM principle doesn't believe in doing for people, but in serving people to do for themselves—giving them dignity and self-determination. Service comes in the form of materials, education, instruction, support, and inspiration. Give a man a fish, and he eats for a day; teach him how to fish, and he eats for life. The adage is true.

The same applied to me. I needed to be with people who encouraged me to do for myself yet didn't abandon me to do everything. I needed people who would give me space to experiment.

Mea's Gift

23

PICK'E'S MOTHER HAD been short lately. I understood she was under stress. Today, Don Pedro wanted a tortilla with garlic because he was still hungry after breakfast. "No. we will have an early lunch," she said.

Mea is overworked. She must do the housework, the cleaning, the shopping, and the cooking; plus, when her husband calls and needs help in the yard, she works with him to rake the leaves. This much responsibility is unjust. I much prefer the modern way of sharing, rather than the woman having a defined role and the man having his. Sharing responsibilities leads to better communication and relationships.

When Mea asked me if I would like to go to the curandero today to use my certificate, I was surprised.

"That sounds great. Thank you," I replied.

"I'll call the curandero for an appointment," she said. "Pick'e will stay with Anna and her family. They have been friends since they were little."

We went to the restaurant near the curandero's office, where we ordered a healthy Mexican vegetable soup, which Mea loves. The waiter brought us each a steaming bowl. Pieces of multicolored bell peppers, red onions, zucchini, corn, black beans, and tomatoes floated at the top, along with the leaves of many herbs. The smells of cumin and oregano invited us to eat. It tasted delicious, with the earthiness of garlic and jalapeños. Scattered around the table were toppings of lime and avocado slices, cilantro, tortilla strips, cheese, and sour cream for us to add. What a delicious, hearty, healthy soup! Mea was right, and we enjoyed our time together.

A block down the street, the curandero's building had a ramp, so Mea rolled me up into the office as Don Pedro held the door. A bent-over old lady approached us as we entered.

"My arthritis is worse today," she said. "My knees hurt like nails when I walk, so I can only do the cards."

When I rolled into the room, the curandero spread the cards out on the bed and dealt them."

"Put your hands on the cards," she said.

As I did, I prayed in my mind, Forgive me, God, because I don't believe in this superstition. But this is a gift, and I don't want to act ungrateful.

She took three sets of cards, cutting them before dealing.

"The first will describe your past life and people who've affected you," she said. We talked about my caring relationships and also some that were not so good. "You have experienced bad luck in love," the curandero concluded. In Mexico, your love life is vital, so it wasn't surprising she said this.

The second pile described a Moreno, a darker person in my life. "He is rich, and occasionally he visits you," she said.

I recognized no Moreno in my life, except maybe Ray.

"This third set will decide if you will get well," she explained.

The curandero laid two cards faced up and said, "Choose one."

One looked like a worm wrapped up with a ribbon; it didn't appeal to me.

The other one showed six coins. I chose that one, although, throughout my life, money wasn't that important; the other repulsed me. This is stupid, I thought, and I asked for forgiveness again.

"You may find help and feel a little better, but you will not rid yourself of this disease," she said. "Sorry. You must live with it as I do with my aches and pains."

Not surprised, I had heard this from everybody. No one had ever said I'd get well—not naturalists, not acupuncturists, and not medical doctors. In my heart, I knew it was true.

But now I was reading a book that promoted a vegetarian diet, raw garlic and drinking lots of lemon and lime juice to reduce inflammation. Don Pedro had been following this diet for several years, and he was much improved. I'm sure it's irrational and illogical, but what will I lose by trying? Nothing.

As anybody with knowledge of nutrition knows, grains and legumes are complete proteins. They are the mainstay in the third world, where access to high-protein foods like meats, eggs, and cheese is often not available. Multigrain tortillas and legumes like lentils and beans are the staff of life here.

I plan to follow the homeopathic diet, and I wrote my affirmations and intentions for the rest of my life:

> ➢ I must learn patience with myself and people who are helping me.

- ➢ I am still alive and somewhat astonished I am. Continue to pray.
- ➢ I need to become more aware of socioeconomic structures that cause inequities and convince others to change them.
- ➢ Get massages.
- ➢ Go to curanderos for more healings.
- ➢ Drink lemon juice with raw garlic many times a day.
- ➢ Eat raw salads with olive oil.
- ➢ Eat almond and oatmeal.
- ➢ Eat peas and other vegetables from non-aluminum cans, if you can't buy fresh.
- ➢ Eat grains and legumes.

24

Watching Pické

PICKÉ HAD PERMISSION to stay with me today. At eleven years old, she wandered off on her own; her father didn't allow her to leave the property without permission. She was riding horseback on a Campesinos horse with one of her girlfriends. After coming back from the curandero, her father saw her half a block down the street as we came around the corner. He got annoyed and grounded her today, so I planned to keep her close.

She was usually an obedient child, considering she was only eleven years old. Pické talked with her friends through her bedroom window but told them she could not come out and play. She was now washing the dishes.

We both had a second breakfast after her parents left because we had such a light one an hour ago. Pické fixed us each a scrambled egg. We had caramelized cream made from goat's milk, which was delicious when spread on our whole wheat bread.

Last time I was here, Pické and I had studied English

together for her exam but had little time to play. I hoped this time would be different.

Seeing the things I had given her displayed made me happy. On a shelf were the postcards my mother had mailed to her to thank her for the birthday and happy Mother's Day letters Pické had written on my behalf. She used multicolor pencils and enjoyed doing so. The Olbas bottle I had given her last Christmas was on the shelf. The books she loved, which I read to her in English and then she translated into Spanish to help me learn her language, were also sitting on the shelf.

On the patio where we ate, it was toasty warm. It was December 29, middle of winter in Wisconsin, and I was barefoot, wearing a skirt and a short-sleeve shirt; I was contented. The sky was blue, with abundant sunshine, and there was just enough cool breeze to keep me comfortable. I was in paradise; I'd died and gone to heaven.

In contrast, in 1986, I had been suicidal. I'd wanted to die. Life had no meaning. I'd felt desolate, neglected, and unsupported. Cuernavaca, its climate, and people had resurrected me. I thought this weather affected the people here positively too.

Pické pointed out the chime carved out of marble with little birds hanging on a fishing line that cling-clanged and chimed together when you hit them or when the wind blew. Seeing the little things I'd given the family being used made me happy.

Last year, I sent Pické a sweater from the Bargain Nook in Mineral Point, which cost me a dollar. It was just beautiful on her, with a rich brown color that matched her hair. She loved it so much she slept in it, turning it inside out because it was so soft inside. Today, she put on one of my old chamois shirts, which turned a light beige color because I'd washed it so many times. Though it was faded and bleached-out now, she still wore it because, she said, once it was mine. I treasured how much this meant to both of us.

25

Celebrating New Year's Eve

TODAY THE SON of the former owner of the house here in Emiliano Zapata rode his palomino and visited with the neighbors. His pride in his stallion mirrored how young US men show off their new cars. I could understand why—what a magnificent horse!

The horse, in many parts of Mexico, was a vehicle for transportation. When a man owns one, he is somebody. I heard horses go by more often than cars or trucks here. The neighbors across the street didn't look wealthy, but they could stable one behind their house wall.

We were celebrating New Year's with a dinner prepared by Inga, a Siberian friend of mine who now lived in Germany. She was making Siberian borage. First, she cooked up oxtail and added chopped up cabbage, onions, tomatoes, potatoes, and carrots. She then boiled the beets, separated the juice, and just before serving the borage, she poured in the beet juice. It was tasty and, I'm sure, healthy with all those vegetables. She made dessert too—a cake frosted with warmed homemade orange marmalade jam.

After dinner, we listened to the music I had brought, including the Chicago Guitar Trio, which everyone enjoyed. At midnight, we toasted each other with tequila, supplied by me to my regret. Instead of firecrackers, men shot their pistols off in the sky to make everyone aware they owned a gun.

Last night, I woke up about 2:00 a.m. when Picke opened my door. She had the smell of alcohol on her breath. She told me she drank some tequila and shared it with her friend Anna.

"I don't feel good," she said. "What should I do, Madrina?"

"You should eat something since you haven't eaten since supper and drink a lot of water," I told her.

Coming back from the kitchen, she climbed into my bed, and we talked for a while. She was only eleven years old. I thought some of her friends gave her the liquor through her window, but she told me the whole story.

"It was the leftover tequila. My mother gave me a little in a cup, and I shared it with my friend Anna."

I wasn't sure this was true, but if it was, it didn't take much to get those two little girls, eleven and fifteen, sick because Picke told me Anna had vomited.

Why had I bought the tequila for the celebration? I couldn't help cook, so I thought maybe I could contribute by bringing something, but I felt guilty.

The incident made me realize what young parents must go through in the States when they worry if their teenagers are doing drugs or drinking.

I am glad Picke trusted and confided in me; I liked to be her co-madre, which meant her mother and I shared motherhood because I was her godmother. Picke didn't want me to tell her parents. Eventually, she would; she always did. But I would wait because I didn't want to break her confidence.

"I am worried that you drank alcohol," I said. "Have you done that before?"

"No. We tried it because everyone else was drinking it," Picke said. "I didn't like the taste."

"Some people can't stop drinking it, and it ruins their lives," I told her. "I don't want that to happen to you."

"I promise I won't drink it again until I'm as old as you," she answered and cried. "Please don't worry."

I held her until she stopped sobbing. "Thank you. I love you, little one," I told her, wiping her tears. As far as I was aware, she didn't drink, and this was her first experience.

Picke's mother was so efficient, she reminded me of mine. She brought me the coffee, and off she would go instead of sitting down and talking with me. Sometimes she made me feel like a burden, the same as with my mother.

In contrast, Sylvia, the mother of my "Mexican family," would sit down, give me a smile, and talk. To her, I was a person first, not just a disabled person. When people were so busy they have no time to talk, one seems like less of a person. In Sylvia's family, I was wanted. I'd stayed here for two weeks; I was packing up in the morning to go back to Cuernavaca and my Mexican family. I missed them.

My two-week stay had added more work onto Mea's shoulders. I could see that she needed a rest.

Who could blame her? We sick people get irritable; it is hard to be dependent. I'm not sure which was worse—caring for a disabled person or being one. If I'd learned anything from this disease, it's, please don't fault the victim. A basic fact is some people need assistance. I believe this was one reason Ray had helped me so much. He recognized that he learned from me— that there are things I could offer him that he could not get anywhere else. I had value. He learned how to minister to the disabled and how we felt about what kind of help we needed.

In America, I felt like a burden. Some people took one look at me and, oh, trouble, they thought and walked away. Even some of my friends slowly distanced themselves over time. People here in Mexico, on the other hand, said they wanted to get to know me. People found value in getting to know someone with disadvantages, someone who was not independent—the American epitome of success.

26

Trouble Back "Home"

WHILE I WAS spending Christmas with the La Paz family, Sylvia's eldest daughter, Magdalena, twenty-five-years- old, returned home. She wanted her bedroom back. I couldn't blame her; this was her home. She had been working in Acapulco in the hospitality business until she'd lost her job when the hotel chain had closed. She hadn't been able to find another job, so she came home.

Finding another place to live might be a good idea at this point. Like a boomerang, I went back and forth on whether I should move to the fuchsia room across from the bathroom without a door or find a new place.

Silvia made healthy foods and grated raw vegetables for me. Her belief and support help me stay on the natural diet and not cheat. It would be hard to be without Juanita; she always helped me with a generous smile. I guessed Magdalena returning would help me decide to move.

The noise level in this house was also getting on my nerves. Perhaps, I had become accustomed to the quiet serenity of the house in Emiliano Zapata. Or maybe my ALS had progressed to a point where I couldn't tolerate noise echoing off the stone walls and concrete floors. After what happened last night, I will be leaving.

I wanted to go to bed at 9:00 p.m., but I couldn't because the TV was on until 11:00 p.m., so I watched TV with the family. What else could I do? When the TV was on, I couldn't concentrate on anything else. At 11:00, they turned it off and said goodnight, and we went to bed. Ah, to sleep, I thought. How peaceful and quiet.

Then the phone rang, and Carlos, the twenty-year-old, answered. He was right outside my room around the corner in the living room on the phone, talking as loudly as if it were broad daylight. For ten minutes, I gritted my teeth and stood it.

"Carlos, please use the phone in your mother's room," I said.

"No. The connection is not good there, Esther. But I will go into the kitchen," he replied.

The kitchen was farther away, but with Carlos continuing to speak as loudly as before, I still couldn't sleep. Carlos kept talking for half an hour or more. I turned on my radio. I put my pillow over my head, but I still heard his loud voice. I turned on my Mozart music loud, and I know it echoed throughout the whole house at a quarter to twelve. By the time I turned it down, he was off the phone; I guess he got the hint. I kept the music on for a while to calm down and took a Valium. Before this episode, I had been so ready for a relaxing sleep at 11:00 p.m.

A few hours of peace to tape my journal was what I needed. I couldn't reason when it was noisy. Nor could I organize my day. Valium would knock me out and give me peace so I could get some sleep, even if medically induced. Maybe I could pass my life this way. Dope up and try to survive, like in the blue room in Mineral Point. Take amphetamines to wake up, antidepressants in the afternoon, and Valium to help me sleep or calm down when needed—anything to help keep me going. Make myself not feel. God bless Valium.

But I didn't want to spend the rest of my shortened life that way, so it was time to find a quieter place to live. My path was a life of adjusting. I was a wandering gypsy, living here, living there, and I never planned it this way. At least, I didn't have to handle snow and ice; storms; and cloudy, drizzling rainy days. It was a little overcast today, and I was tired because I didn't sleep well last night. I had to adjust to many things here, but at least I need not adapt to the weather.

I said nothing this morning about the issue from last night, and nobody else did either. Most of the family said, "Good morning, Esther," and Sylvia gave me a hug and a smile as she put a steaming bowl of oatmeal in front of me. Carlos didn't say a word.

27

My New Home

I FOUND A house closer to CCIDD in a charming neighborhood, and now I lived with an American woman writer, Judith. I rented a large room with a bathroom and a closet with shelves in her home. Having my private bath was liberating. For months, I'd had to shove my items in a plastic bag or keep them in a cardboard box by my bed. With places for my things now, I could roll into the bathroom, and find all my things where I had put them. It sounds a little childlike, but this meant a sense of stability to me.

I had a desk overlooking my favorite part—glass windows from floor to ceiling with a sliding door inviting me out to the lawn and beyond to the world. I was paying eight dollars per day, but I would shop and pick out my own food.

My rental included the maid, Salina, but she didn't approve of this. At first, she'd been helpful, getting vegetables out of the refrigerator so I could make soup, but I was having trouble with her now. When you were in charge, you could do things as you liked them done. But when someone else worked for you, who said how the task should be done? One example was that I preferred my lettuce sliced small so I could easily chew it, which could be a problem for me. When I asked Salina to please prepare my salad that way, she replied, "We don't do it that way. We peel off the leaves."

Just because she was doing this for me, Salina assumed she could do things the way she wanted. I needed an equal voice in how things were done, but I didn't think equality existed in this kind of relationship. One was always dominating another, and I was tired of being controlled because I was disabled and dependent. Worry about who would feed me breakfast, lunch, and dinner was always on my mind. I'd like to take these things for granted so I could go on to other work that captured my spirit, like my book.

Caretakers often wanted just to keep you alive, but disabled persons need a reason to live beyond their physical needs. We want the world to be a better place when we leave it, just like others do. We can be of service to others with help and moral support. I know someday I will need someone to feed me. I'm hoping to God that I don't have to die a slow incapacitating, deteriorating condition of death—the usual outcome of Lou Gehrig's disease.

Being handicapped is a different journey. To wake up every morning in a degenerating body is challenging and depressing. Some people don't want to be around a person with such tremendous issues. It means obligation; someone will need your help. They will ask favors of you. Better stay away. Don't go near them. Then you won't get entangled in the obstacles they represent because they're sitting in a wheelchair with withering hands and feet.

Since I developed ALS, some people just quietly exited my life—not because I asked too much of them, but because of what my disease implies. It isn't comfortable to be around me because of my condition. I am the symbol of dependency. Limited as I am, I represent the antithesis of what US society admires.

I know I can be assertive, but I am always pushing on a wall. My mind puts up many barriers—things I think I can't do, which I can. Society tries to tell me what I should and shouldn't do with my disability, confined to a wheelchair. So every day, I get up fighting those walls, and this makes me pushy.

Some caretakers try to put you in a dependent role. You fight it because you want to be equal even though you are dependent. Maybe you are putting your caretaker in a role because you are asking him or her to help you. Yet you are trying to exert independence and individuality to keep up your self-esteem. The situation is full of contradictions, and you are struggling inside to stay who you have always been, despite your disabilities.

Nicaragua is working toward self-determination but yet depends on other countries coming to her aid. The international community needs to know how to relate in a way where the Nicaraguan people can maintain their self-esteem.

The roses outside had all opened, and this place was so bright and tranquil, every dawn renewed me. I loved the quiet; I could think. The first week I was here, my skull was still reverberating from the memory of the constant noise and the disco-rock radio music that echoed off the concrete walls in Sylvia's house.

Memories flooded back—of when I was twenty years old, how I'd loved to dance to the music of the '50s, the loud rock and roll music like Mack the Knife, Elvis Presley, or Fats Domino. I recognized a generation gap of my own. Carlos loved the music just like I did, and I couldn't expect him not to play it, so I moved. I needed peace for more time during the day. Living with Sylvia helped me realize that I couldn't continue to live with a family; I wanted more control.

Ideally, I wanted my place, with employees who I could hire or fire if they weren't compatible. This would allow me more choice in who would help me.

Silvia and Juanita were exceptional helpers. But it was time to leave, with the return of their eldest daughter, and Carlos needing his space.

Few families wanted this burden. I was a burden; the rare human being exists with the needed values and compassion for a situation like this.

How could I feel joy in a wheelchair? It was impossible unless sometimes I was doing what I wanted to do, what I was called to do. Moving to Mexico was the right thing for me. I was still alive and had ended up in this paradise.

Because of the solitude this morning, I could write a letter to a teenage boy we raised at The Wooden Shoe while I was living there:

> Dear Rain,
> A little birdie told me you are having a tough time, and I wanted to give you some advice. It is so easy to fault others for your problems, but that won't improve your life. I experienced this as I was trying to blame my mother, and she was blaming me for getting Lou Gehrig's disease. Feeling guilty about

trivial things because they may have caused my condition is fruitless. It is absurd to feel responsible when one gets a devastating illness.

It is easy to criticize oneself, friends, family, community, or even the weather. Much more meaningful is to work on improving yourself and cultivate compassion for yourself and others. I believe until one learns to forgive and sympathize with oneself, it is hard to be helpful to others. How one treats oneself is how one is with other people.

Sometimes, kindness seems of limited value in our culture. Often, others make well-meaning people feel they are too softhearted or foolish when they get involved. In the United States, one learns to be tough, independent, and individualistic, which may not be compatible with having compassion. But, throughout history, all the faiths and religions valued caring for others, and I hope you will too. I wish the best for you and that you have a happy and fulfilling life.

Love,
Esther

Sometimes I missed The Wooden Shoe and the people who were my "family" for three years of my life. As I pondered this, looking out the window, the sun was sinking below the horizon; I saw the great variety of trees on the property. There was a eucalyptus tree with its trunk all twisted before the branches spread and reached for the sky. Another tree looked like a spruce tree but was a tropical evergreen. The interesting trees together made a lovely picture silhouetted against the setting sun.

28

The Wooden Shoe

AFTER WRITING TO the child raised at The Wooden Shoe, I was nostalgic for the life I'd spent as an alternative to living in traditional families. We had wanted to try a different way as pioneers living together.

But how had this commune begun? A little history will help here. Antiwar students from Dartmouth College realized the ROTC program was training officers to go to Vietnam and kill. These activists launched a campaign to remove the ROTC from the campus and took over the administration building. The police arrested and jailed some of them in the same facility. When they gained their freedom, they talked about living together. When released, a member of the group rented a house in Vermont. Many of the protesters moved into the house. This was the beginning.

As the group grew, they searched Vermont and New Hampshire, looking for a property. A beat-up abandoned 1790s farmhouse in Canaan, New Hampshire, seemed promising. They borrowed $1,000 from a Dartmouth professor for a down payment, and one member of the group borrowed the rest from his parents. They bought the farm in 1970.

A child was born about the time they moved into the farmhouse. The dilapidated farmhouse had no running water—a problem that required some collective brainpower to solve. First, they dug a trench and laid a pipe, so the water flowed into the basement by gravity from the well. Hand pumping brought the water up into the sink. Without electricity, kerosene lamps provided light. A cast-iron potbelly stove served as a heating source and for cooking. There was no phone.

Everyone took turns with the chores. One member conceived of hiring out to help a woman who had lost her husband. She lived in a big farmhouse and didn't want to leave, but she had nobody to maintain the house. The roof needed fixing, or she needed wood chopped to heat the house for the winter and no way of getting any. The Wooden Shoe Labor Force was formed. A crew of well-educated, articulate persons would arrive and do odd jobs in the community for those in need like the recent widow. Collectively they planted tulip bulbs, tore down buildings, planted gardens, shoveled snow, raked leaves, and painted lots of old barns and sheds. Two older women gave all of their late husband's tools to the force.[1]

In June 1971, I joined The Wooden Shoe. I remember most the long meetings, some lasting for twelve hours, where we discussed money, planned for the force jobs, and made a list of who would help with which chore on each day. Pigs, chickens, and our cow, Sophie, all needed attention.

Everyone agreed that nobody would have a regular job, as

---

[1] Shelby Grantham, "The Wooden Shoe: A Commune," *Dartmouth Alumni Magazine* (May 1976), 29 –35.

a regular job would prevent us from being available to cook or take care of the children enough of the time. We raised two children collectively; both were born at the commune. All of us learned how to take care of the children. We changed diapers, fed them, and encouraged them to play together. They received love from many people. If the commune dissolved, everyone knew the children would go with their biological parents, so we learned to compromise.

During our meetings, everyone discussed what was on his or her mind, hashing out the complexities of our relationships. We charted new territory, being the only collective farm where the breaking down of gender roles was a shared goal. We all, women and men, took turns roofing, planting and harvesting crops, canning, working outside the commune in the workforce, and cooking. The best cook was a guy.

To illustrate that there was no bias to our gender in assigning work, here's a typical work schedule for me. One week, I learned how to work with both a Slant-Six and an older Flathead-Six, Dodge engine, when Ben came for a visit. Another week, I went haying four times at Bryson's Farm. The next day, we hitchhiked to Rutland, Vermont, to pick peaches. And when we'd finished, six of us loaded 9,000 pounds of wheat into a truck; each bag weighed 120 pounds. As one member said, "Your genitalia doesn't matter."

After our meeting on Sunday, here is my work schedule until next Monday.

Monday	Work at the dump
Tuesday	Clean and freeze peaches
Wednesday	Prepared the soil for potatoes

Thursday	Paint at Katz Farm 7-7
Friday	My laundry and watch the children
Saturday	Extract honey
Sunday	Planning meeting and cooking
Monday	Care for animals and milk Sophie

During one meeting, someone said, "Esther, you are a fair, honest listener who gets to the heart of the problem and puts out positive energy."

I felt appreciated, as I belonged to the earth and people of all ages who farmed the land. We tilled the soil by hand with a hoe, weeded vegetables on our hands and knees, and loved it.

My favorite jobs were caring for the children and milking Sophie, our cow. I volunteered for these. While milking Sophie, the memories of the goats we'd had when I was young came into my mind. Making yogurt and cheese were my specialties.

We raised most of our food. Someone found an old root cellar buried in the ground, where our harvested potatoes, carrots, squashes, onions, and apples stayed fresh over the frigid New England winters.

We used to joke about how long we could stay put if the world ended, and we figured at least a month with no contact. We all smoked cigarettes, so I don't know how we thought we would last without smokes for even one day.

Being vegetarians, I remember myself, and another guy would make ourselves scarce when slaughter time came. The experience was traumatic. Raising the pig, sometimes giving it a name, created a bond, and now we had to kill it to provide food for ourselves. Our neighbor allowed us to use his freezer space for our meat, and we helped pay his electric bill. Bartering was a great way to do business at The Wooden Shoe.

All of us were skinny, with not much fat, and when the carnivores went into town to do the laundry, they would gobble down greasy hamburgers from the local fast-food joint.

My friend Odessa and I helped each other through some difficult times. Odessa considered me her child's surrogate mother. I cherished the time I spent with him. By this time, I had decided I didn't want children of my own; something called me to be an activist in a way that wouldn't leave much quality time for a child. If I had a baby, I would want to devote all my time to raising my son or daughter, and I realized I couldn't do both.

I found a poem I had saved entitled "A Good Mother" by Louise Pugh Corder, which helped reinforce my belief that I wouldn't have children. I believed with all my heart that the poem states the truth about a good mother, and I couldn't be both a good mother and an activist.

29

Visiting the Botanical Gardens

I TRAVELED TO the Botanical Herb Gardens, looking for the stinging nettle Dr. Rodrigues recommended. The taxi driver turned in the wrong direction on an inclined street, and we found ourselves at a dead end. When I urged the driver to stop and ask a man on the street where the herb garden was, he told me the man wouldn't know. A few blocks later, I saw two schoolgirls walking down the street. Since they looked as if they lived in the neighborhood, I called out to them. "I'm looking for the herb garden?" I said.

"Two blocks up and one to the left," they said.

I thanked them, and the cab driver drove me there, brought my chair out, and helped me up on the sidewalk.

"That will be 2,500 pesos," he said.

"If you get me down those two steps," I said, "I'll give you 3,000 pesos" ($1.50).

Rolling myself on the path, I proceeded along the steep

walkway in my wheelchair with the brakes on and dragging my feet. I called out to a man nearby, "Will you please help me?"

Thinking I was out of control, he blocked the chair and stopped my progress.

"This is the way I break on a steep incline," I said, adding, "I need help to get down to that lower level, please."

He and another man accompanying him carried me in my wheelchair.

"Thank you for your help."

Rolling myself along the path, I saw a variety of trees. The mango came from Asia and the coffee bean tree from Africa. A sign at the base of each tree or plant gave its proper name, origin, and botanical or Latin nomenclature, along with the Spanish term and its uses. A variety of herbs grew along the walkway. Because it was the dry season, the plants looked dusty, although someone watered them. I would come here again during the rainy season to see it when it was lush and green.

I came over a narrow stone bridge, so I turned my chair backward to wheel myself up, using my feet. Moving off to one side of the bridge, I realized my tire was only a few inches from the edge, ready to go over the embankment into the black water. I stopped in time before the wheel ran off the edge of the bridge. Turning myself around, I continued over the bridge frontward and rolled along the incline on the other side.

A creeping vine intertwined with other plants in the woods. Large white blossoms on the vine helped me identify the plant as the flora passionada. The leaves are an herb I take that helps to prevent cramped muscles so I can relax before bedtime. Fennel plants were huge, and I imagined their delicious underground bulbs cut up in an orange salad or cooked as they are in Europe.

A few bamboos had hearts with names etched into them; one could imagine the young lovers standing by the trees as they carved their initials.

I asked the gardener, "Where is the stinging nettle, please?"

"Over there," he said, pointing. He pushed me around the garden, showing me different plants, but none of them looked like the one I needed. I described those found around old barns in Wisconsin and at the Wooden Shoe, the kind the Naturista doctor had said I should use for lashing my skin.

"We find those in the hills and mountains during the rainy season, but we don't grow them in these gardens."

Because he was friendly, I asked him, "I need help to go to the museum, please."

He helped turn my chair backward on the stairs in the proper way, tipping the chair back and bringing the wheels down one step at a time. Most people need instructions, but he naturally did it.

He said, "Okay. It's flat for the rest of the way, so you should be fine."

I thanked him for his help, and he told me to have fun at the museum.

What a pleasant afternoon, learning at my pace with no one in a hurry to do something else. I imagined if a friend had taken me to the museum, he or she might have become bored and said, "Let's go."

Needing a ride home, I would have left. My friend might not have considered whether I wanted to stay longer, so I enjoyed coming alone today.

I took my time reading the different plaques next to each dried herb encased in glass. Large displays showed names and samples of herbs known to be helpful to the circulatory, nervous, and endocrine systems and the skin, muscles, and bones. I copied the list of the herbs used for muscles and the nervous systems.

The shop girl helped me so I could visit the museum gift shop. I bought a jar of honey and a small delicate basket before she closed.

"Where could I get a taxi?" I asked her.

"I'll help you find one," she replied.

She pushed me up to the corner where we could watch for a cab. I prepared to wait, but one came around the corner within a few minutes and pulled over to the curb and stopped.

The driver helped me into the front seat and stored my wheelchair in the trunk. I asked if the shop girl needed a ride, and she said she lived close by and enjoyed the walk. I thanked her for being so helpful and prepared for the trip home.

The cab drivers gave me mobility; they were my unique needs caravan. Cuernavaca has such caring cab drivers, who charge what the bus costs in the States, only a dollar or two. If I tip thirty cents, they will help me with stairs or through a door. This wheelchair has been in the back seats or trunks of many taxis since I have been here. These cab drivers created a tremendous difference in my lifestyle.

30

Wanting More Control

I NEEDED MORE control of my life, so I looked at a studio apartment near where I'd lived with Sylvia's family. The best part was its location—next to the park where I used to sit and imagine how delightful living in this neighborhood would be. The studio apartment was furnished with a covered terrace, screened porch, and a garden; the garden was smaller than where I lived now, but it had a gardener's care. However, without a telephone, I would have to depend on friends. Ray thought the place too small—that I might become claustrophobic. I was ready to not be at the mercy of the person living with me— whether my mother or the maid at Judith's place, who may lose patience with my disease. Every day, Lou Gehrig's made demands on me; there was no choice.

I rented the studio apartment and hired a girl named Lula to help me on days when I had things I must do. Today, she cut my hair and cleaned the apartment. She gave me great support, and I liked her cheery disposition—essential to my psychological and physical well-being. I thought I was paying her well, in the hope that she'd stay with me.

Lula filled my water jug from the outdoor faucet, which comes from the well; I boiled the kitchen tap water as it comes from the holding tank, which had stagnant water and was questionable.

I heard that last year in Managua, Nicaragua, the water became contaminated; I thought of what a devastating blow to their revolution and the people. When I lived in Managua, the water was so clean everybody drank it from the faucet; no one got sick.

Lula came this evening and pushed me up the hill so I could hire a cab to go to CCIDD and meet with people who make me feel important. After chatting a while about how to handle the largest group of church members from the United States and Canada that were coming to visit next week, I asked one of the staff to please push me out the back door.

"I'm fine here," I said. "But please leave the door open in case the driver forgets to pick me up at 9:00 p.m."

He hadn't come at a quarter to ten, so I reasoned I would give him ten more minutes, and then I would flag down one of the many cabs buzzing by on the street. I'd rolled my chair to the end of the sidewalk and was sitting in my wheelchair alone when two young boys pulled up in their car. They said they were brothers, and we talked until I felt at ease. My intuition told me they were okay. They asked if I needed a ride; I said I sure would appreciate one, so they helped me settle in the front seat and stored my wheelchair in the trunk. They drove me, and when we got to my door, I pretended the people I lived with wouldn't be back until midnight. I handed them the keys, and they helped me open the door and rolled me into the apartment. I tipped them and thanked them for stopping for me.

Sometimes, I was lonely living alone, but the positive part was that I was more relaxed now than I'd been in years. Lying on the bed, right next to the window, I could look out on the terrace with the white wicker-looking lawn furniture, which was actually plastic, with waterproof blue seat cushions.

The rain was coming, the second significant rain we'd had after six months of no rain. The pitter-patter of the drops on the roof was pleasant to hear. I was so close to the window; I almost felt like I was outside.

The rain made me think of a memory of meeting Tomas in Fort Myers, Florida. He came in from the orange grove, dripping wet from an all-day deluge and a bag of oranges he had been picking slung over his shoulder. The torrents of rain were dripping off the brim of his hat. I had been picking strawberries and was waiting under a tent for the bus to take me back to my living quarters in Fort Myers. When it came, we all got on the bus, and Tomas sat next to me. We talked, and I noticed bloody scratches on his arms and hands. He saw me staring.

"The spines on the orange trees scratch my arms," he said.

"Ouch!" I replied. My imagination went wild when he told me how he drove the tractor when the rain came down so hard the field flooded, and he had to plow through a wall of water and almost got swept away.

"I saved the tractor and the wagon of filled orange crates," he said.

When we returned to our living complex, the kids in the neighborhood ran up to him, yelling, "Oranges, oranges." Tomas gave all the children an orange. They went away with a smile and juice running down their chins. I got one, too— delicious. Funny what you think about when it rained.

With the rain, I thought I would fall asleep like I had when I was a child, but my mind kept going back to Tomas and the time I'd spent in the African American community in Fort Myers as I wanted to escape from "white America" during one of my manic episodes. Sensing something was wrong, though not knowing I already had early symptoms of Lou Gehrig's disease, I'd become tight with my money.

Tomas asked me to lend a man he knew five dollars and introduced me to him. "Esther, this is Harold. He repairs roofs around here."

Harold looked to be in his late fifties and came straight from work, dressed in overhauls smudged with tar. I held out my hand to shake Harold's, but he drew his hand back. "Sorry, Esther. My hands are dirty. Been working with steaming tar all day," he said.

"That's okay," I said and shook his hand.

"This is just a loan," I said as I handed him five dollars. "I want you to repay the money when you are able."

He smiled, nodded his head yes, and left.

"He will never pay you back," Tomas said.

But on the weekend, on payday, Harold came back and laid a five-dollar bill in my hand. A little girl about six or seven years old hid behind Harold and tightly gripped his hand. He introduced her as his granddaughter, Chavela.

"What a beautiful name, Chavela," I said. "Would you like to play with my magic markers?" I laid a few pieces of paper on the table and drew circles using various colors.

She came over and sat down by me to color without saying a word. Chavela drew a rainbow in a blue sky using all the colors. When Chavela left, she smiled at me. To this day, I regret taking back that five-dollar bill. It was my introduction to the third world right here in the United States, and my eyes were blind.

I lived in Fort Myers, Florida, for a time with Tomas while I was working in the vegetable gardens. Con games were standard. I didn't get angry with the people. This was how it was at the bottom of the economic ladder and at the top too. It was just more "legal" when the corporations did it because they hired expensive lawyers who kept them out of trouble.

One night, Tomas said something about her pretty dress to a white woman whose husband owned the store down the street. The husband got angry. And Tomas came back, slammed the door, and said, "Esther, "I'm in trouble."

As he finished telling me what happened, the room shook from someone's' fists pounding against the door.

"What do you want?" I said.

An angry man burst through the door and lunged at Tomas. I tried to pull him off, and after a few punches, he quit.

"Tomas explained this to me. I think there has been a misunderstanding," I said. "He has never bothered anyone since I've known him. I don't care what anybody says, he never would do that."

I stood up for Tomas, and so did the neighborhood. Many boycotted the store, and via the grapevine, the word got around. The store owner came to talk to the owner of our complex, and I overheard him through an open window.

"I'm losing hundreds of dollars because of this," he said.

"There is nothing I can do," our apartment manager said. "Perhaps you should apologize."

The next day he apologized and gave Tomas $150. Tomas knew I liked to watch television, so he bought a used big screen TV.

31

Mother Wants to Come and Visit

RENTING MY PLACE brought a deep relaxation I hadn't had for a long time. Sitting outside in the garden with the birds chirping and the barn-red wall where the flowers intertwined gave me so much peace and hope I could improve my condition. My left foot seemed to be firmer; I could use it more. Maybe it was my imagination. I wouldn't know until things were more obvious. Living by myself and hiring my help added to my relief. With my added energy, I could shop, keep myself clean, organize my kitchen, cook, feed myself, and wash the dishes.

Today, Mother and Regina would call me from California. I'd made plans to go to my friend Marcy's house to receive the call at five o'clock this evening. With plenty of time to pick up my mail at the post office, I rolled from one barrio through the archway into the alleyway by my friend's house. Maneuvering my wheelchair was difficult because of a two-foot grade from the alleyway up to the sidewalk. I'd learned to ask when I needed help. Two well-dressed young girls looking like they had come from church said they would help me. People in Latin America consider it a privilege to help those in need. This idea is ingrained in their culture, and that makes me realize I am home.

When I got to Marcy's I heard the phone ringing inside at 5:00 p.m.; I knew my mother was calling. Marcy had locked her door; I couldn't answer, so I went shopping. A little way up the street, I recognized Carlos, Pablo, and Sylvia's son. We exchanged our subdued greetings; I guess we both were holding somewhat of a grudge.

Realizing this, I stopped and said, "Please say hello to your parents and little sister, Juanita, Carlos." Then I rolled on toward the farmer's market.

On the way, I met the mother of Lula, the girl who I hired to cut my hair and clean my apartment. Chatting for a while, I told her how pleased I was with her daughter working for me, always with a smile. At the market, I bought mangoes, bananas, milk, and chili peppers—the kind that wasn't too hot. A little spice was okay, but I always removed the seeds where the heat lies.

Lula's mother pushed me back to Marcy's house, just as she was getting home.

"Oh, Esther, I'm so sorry. I forgot your mother was calling today," Marcy said.

As we were trying to figure out what to do next, Vicki, Marcy's daughter, came unto the porch and said, "Esther, your mother's on the phone."

I talked with my mother and Regina. Regina's son wanted to see the ballet of Alice in Wonderland in San Francisco, so they didn't have long to talk. I wished I could go too.

Regina said she wanted to come and visit me in Cuernavaca and bring Kenny.

"With two beds in my room, I would love to have you stay with me," I said.

Feeling obligated to invite my mother, I invited her for a week's vacation. She said maybe later, and I heaved a sigh of relief.

But the next week when I received a call from my mother at Marcy's, she had changed her mind.

"I want to come to visit you," she said. "I'll come for a month."

Oh no, not a whole month, I thought.

"I only invited you for a week," I said. "CCIDD has a project; they need my help."

"I'll stay somewhere else then," she said. "I'll stay with your Mexican family."

"Mother, no. They don't have room since their eldest daughter came back home. Stay with me for a week," I said.

As soon as she hung up, the panic started. A Valium calmed me down. But after I'd had my coffee, the panic began again.

One of the curanderos had said that maybe one of my parents was causing my problems, and I believed this may be partially true. The panic my mother's visit created is an example of how I overreacted to her continuing to insist on staying a month when I wanted her to stay one week. If I was honest, I wasn't sure I could handle that much time with her.

Talking with my therapist, I attempted to release deep-seated tension accumulated over many years. She asked, "What are you experiencing, Esther?"

"Anger and hurt," I said.

"Toward whom do you have these emotions?" my therapist asked.

I told her the feelings weren't directed toward my brothers or sisters or my father and not even toward Orlando, the guy I'd lived with for three years in Europe before the romance ended. I realized I felt these emotions toward my mother. Her lack of responsiveness toward me caused these emotions, like with the blue room. She had taken three years to respond to my request to paint it a more cheerful shade. Regina had painted her daughter's walls within two weeks when she'd wanted to change the color.

Once we moved to the United States, the only adult besides my father in my life was my mother. All our uncles and aunts lived in Switzerland; they seldom visited us. With a lack of connection with my mother but a close relationship with my father, I now sought male friends more than I did female friends.

Absolute panic was setting in, and I must tell my mother not to come. I was unprepared to have her in my life again. The eight years I'd lived with her had been an ordeal. When I'd tried to explain how I felt about wanting to live in Mexico because I couldn't cope living there in the United States, she'd looked at me with this look of either non-comprehension or disbelief.

We didn't trust each other. My mother wanted to make me over, change me, and control me. She didn't respect my right to be free to choose my values and live my life.

What did I have in common with my mother? Had she gone through the trials, despair, and finally finding hope as I had? I didn't think my mother could relate to that; she had experienced nothing like it. Not like Nicaragua, where every year another devastation comes, and the people must cope.

I remembered sitting in the blue room in Mineral Point, taking antidepressants, taking speed, taking Valium just to make it through another day because I was so overwhelmed. If only I hadn't needed to cope with all the ups and downs and only had Lou Gehrig's disease, it would have been so much easier.

After meeting Ray and living out my dreams in Cuernavaca and Nicaragua, I felt free of the psychological burden.

The thought of my mother coming here brought up all those emotions again. Maybe I needed to examine them? I didn't know. I would rather just forget and realize it was impossible to solve—to know the things I could not change and just let go of the rest. Yet, I could try to understand and work through this relationship with my mother in a manner of compassion, not anger and resentment. Maybe this was God's work we must do here on earth to get closer to him. When I asked for help, and someone did so with a smile, I felt God was supporting me through that person.

My biggest fear was not death. I feared most to be alone again, suffering, isolated, and forgotten, without Ray or someone who understood me.

The worst would be an oppressive personality living in the same house as me. I didn't want to live with my mother. When I lived in Mineral Point with her, I felt like a failure because I had Lou Gehrig's disease. I was a failure because I was disabled; that was how I felt around my mother. She was well and healthy in her seventies; she'd succeeded in raising a family. I had failed because, before the age of fifty, I was in a wheelchair, disabled, and living on Social Security. What had I accomplished? What value did I have, if any?

I tried to tell her how I felt; it didn't appear to mean anything to her. She said she didn't believe me, or she thought someone else had put the idea in my head. My mother treated me like an inconsequential dependent, not a complete person.

32

Mother's Visit

NOT WANTING TO hurt my mother by telling her not to come, I decided I would make the best of it. She arrived two days ago, and yesterday we attended a Mass to celebrate solidarity with Nicaragua on the tenth anniversary of the Sandinista Revolution. People from the base community and clergy from Cuernavaca took part in the celebration.

We sang Nicaraguan church songs. Several people from the community read passages from the Bible, which said, "If you love God but hate your neighbor, then you are a liar. If you love God, you also love your neighbor." I didn't connect Nicaragua with being our neighbor in the United States. When you think of a neighbor, you often think of someone in your vicinity, not some country thousands of miles away. But the world is so small today. Nicaragua is our neighbor. It seems no matter what we do to help Nicaragua, it is never enough compared to how much we spend on ourselves.

We went out for lunch and spent twenty thousand pesos; we will go out to dinner with Ray at the Hacienda Cortez tonight, another thirty thousand pesos. Considering how much

I will sacrifice and what I spend on myself, gives me pause as I measure it against my desire to be of service.

An old Mexican man told a story at the celebration. "I was visiting a friend in Nicaragua," he said. "As the sun went down and the sky turned dark, I told my friend I would go down to the cafe on the corner for a coffee.

"I was walking back alone when the police stopped me. My first reaction was to be on guard because, in Mexico, you never know what the police will do. The Nicaraguan police asked if they could help.

"'No. I'm visiting a friend, and I went out for coffee.'

"They realized I was not a Nica because of my accent and walked me home. The way the policeman treated me with respect moved me."

Ray asked me to speak of my experiences in Nicaragua, so I spoke of how important it was for me to go there as part of my struggle.

"Meeting the disabled filled me with sadness," I said. "I am sorry to know my government is doing this to Nicaragua, causing so much suffering and crucifying a whole nation. I hope God will shed light on the US government, so the people of the United States will realize what they are doing and will be with the Nicaraguans forever," I said with tears gathering in my eyes.

The next day, my mother and I wanted to attend a fiesta in Samopasopa, a small village southwest of Cuernavaca. The only way to get that high on the mountain is a yellow twenty-six passenger bus. Green corn plants grew among the rocks. Oak trees and mountain cedar decorated the treacherous road going up the mountain.

What if we met a large Coca-Cola truck coming down the road? I thought. It was a new stone road, narrow, no shoulder. I was sitting by the window, and below me was a precipice of a ravine. We were inches from death. Just a foot, and down we'd go, tumbling over and over into this deep gorge!

The group from the bus came to meet their relatives, and I stayed down near the doctor's office with my mother.

"I need some time alone," I said. "I'll be back in a while."

Sitting under a tree by myself, I felt guilty. The fiesta was taking place above in the churchyard. Only men appeared to be at the fiesta, so I didn't want to go, even though the opportunity came up when two North Americans came up the path and asked if I wanted them to push me up the hill.

The native women were selling woven baskets and approached me to buy one. I tried to open my coin purse but couldn't, as my hands would not cooperate. I expressed my frustration in Spanish. An older woman picked up the coin purse and opened it for me. She smiled at me.

"God has given us the gift of our hands to weave beautiful baskets. Surely he has given you other gifts," she said.

Her affirmative words were what I knew my life had become. I could no longer be the activist I was, but I could translate activism into my book.

I sat underneath the laurel tree, which was way above me on the plaza, and as I was below a twenty-foot wall, I could only see up the stairway to the fiesta.

I didn't see many animals; women carried water in clay pots on their backs held on by ropes. A young boy about ten years old carried a thick stick over his shoulders with two buckets of water, one on each side for balance.

The poverty of the village was visible in the patched and torn clothing they wore.

Most of the villager's clothing was dark grey, blue, or black, except a young girl dressed in a bright pink cape.

I was sitting alone when a young boy showed me a tortilla basket and asked if I would buy it for four thousand pesos. I sensed he was in need, so I gave him five thousand pesos. He took it, said, "Muchas gracias," and ran fast, straight to his home.

The village women approached me to sell their baskets, and when they found I spoke Spanish, about twenty young women and girls surrounded me. I couldn't resist buying from this young girl with yellowish eyes. She tried so hard to sell me some baskets, so I bought one for three thousand pesos. Another young girl was selling round baskets with a cover decorated with delicate fresh flowers, which I purchased for four thousand pesos.

When I returned, the doctor was sitting with my mother. We talked a while. He worked for the government in health clinics, where he stayed for six months. If people couldn't afford the medicine, the government provided it for free, if there was any. They must divide the medication, and only a certain amount was available for each Mexican state; the different villages must share.

We commented on the van that was selling potato chips in bright-colored aluminum foil packets. Women in their shawls clustered around, holding out large plastic bags. The man dumped in little bags of potato chips. Maybe they sold them from their houses to the villagers.

There was a sign outside a store: "Drink or enjoy Coca-Cola." Coca-Cola was everywhere, so were potato chips. To buy a bright shiny aluminum foil bag of potato chips made one feel happy like something good was happening in one's life, especially living a dreary life in such poverty.

Samopasopa had a little bus going up from Taxco, and now they had three roads; twenty years ago, they had no way to go. I wanted to stay there for several days. It was like my disease was irrelevant here. What was important to the people of Samopasopa? Maybe they developed a human community, a place to belong with people like themselves.

My mother wanted to go for a walk around Cuernavaca today, but she had to go alone, as I was falling asleep and needed a nap. I used up too much energy at the fiesta yesterday. I gave her directions to the American-English Library and the bank where she could exchange some money.

"You can walk through town on your mission to find someone who needs the coat you brought from the States," I said. "There are several restaurants where you could stop for lunch. I will take a nap until about two o'clock this afternoon," I said. "I need to be alone."

I felt churning inside because she was wrapping herself in a cocoon to insulate herself. She didn't like to see me upset, thinking it was harmful to my health.

But not feeling emotions made me feel dead inside. If you couldn't handle the deep emotions in one spectrum, how could you feel them in another? The depths of the sadness were reflected in the depths of the gladness. It is to be human.

***

My mother left on August 1, and I missed her. I rolled over in bed this morning and called "Mother." I wasn't awake and forgot she left yesterday.

It was hard being with her; I felt confused and full of contradictions. I thought she resented me getting my disease and for not being what she had hoped. Maybe this was the way I felt around her. So many other people admired my stamina and courage, so it was confusing. But when you had a fatal disease, you needed a mother. You needed comfort, and when your mother wasn't there—didn't comfort—even though she was alive and present, it was hard to take. I found comfort and compassion from other people.

I was feeling lonely; I missed Mineral Point and New Hampshire people. Humans are always looking for greener pastures. They never seem satisfied, or maybe it was just me. My biggest frustration was not being able to get up and walk to the bathroom, while my seventy-four-year-old mother walked a mile and a half through the center of town. Maybe part of the problem was I was jealous, knowing I'd never walk again, knowing I may degenerate further, and I'd be more dependent on other people. On who? Who would take care of me? I must surrender again to God. Yes, I would miss my mother for a while, even though she got on my nerves. I got emotionally and physically worn out with my mother here. We did a lot of activities, going to the Cuernavaca Center a few days and out to lunch and dinner at the Haçienda Cortez with Ray. I am most tired because of going to the Fiesta at Samopasopa.

One must eventually make peace with death. You know it is down the road, just not where or when. If you are afraid of death, you are fearful of life. When you conquer your fear, it can become an inspiration for your life, the kind you talk about with Jesus. To believe life goes beyond the grave helps you live on this side.

33

Survival and Distraction

I AM LYING out on the blanket I bought when my mother and I went to the festival. All the colors and schemes are all wrong, all clashing colors; none of them match. Such a jumble, and I love it. It looks like the artist used all leftover yarns and wove a blanket. The handmade tag says made of wool, but I'm not sure I believe it. It is soft and light and perfect for lying out on the grass or at the beach. The blanket weaver was a tall indigenous Mexican from Higado.

I've been thinking of what it will take to finish my book. Survival takes you from one day to the next and doesn't allow you to look too many days ahead. You stay in the present, taking one day at a time—contrary to the discipline one needs to write a book. A book implies a future, and a book requires planning where you don't allow distractions.

While in survival, your psyche needs distraction once someone takes care of your physical needs, so you don't focus on your disease. Wherever you find a pleasant diversion to uplift you, you do it. You take advantage of it and enjoy it. You nurture a kind of personality that thrives on distraction.

Now I am in this studio apartment, which is deluxe, with a well-kept lawn and gardens. Things are comfortable, so I am trying to change and become disciplined to write my book. This is a significant change, where you seek to not yield to distraction but concentrate on one thing. If I can focus for one hour when writing a letter or reading a book, I'm doing well. What a challenge, but I will write this book at my pace and on my timeline.

34

My Vendors

I HAVE WANTED ice cream, and today I have a little square on a cookie in my freezer. The vendor on the street was calling out selling his product, he sounds like a duck quacking. He has an incredible sense of humor. He was an ugly-looking man, but the light inside him dispels it all.

"What happened to you?" he asked me.

"It's a disease," I told him.

I looked at his deformed hand, which I noticed last time I saw him. "What happened to your hand?" I asked.

"I broke the bones in it a while back; they are sticking out, but they still work," he said. He socked himself playfully in the jaw to prove it.

"Well, I don't want to fight with you," I said with a giggle.

We both laughed. Three little children came up to his cart to buy ice cream. I bought two ice cream sandwiches; they were homemade. I ate one of the ice cream sandwiches and will put the other in the freezer.

I'm not afraid to eat a lot of street food anymore. Yesterday, I had hard-shell tacos at the market. First, they spread sour cream and then sprinkled cheese and garnished with tomatoes, onions, and cilantro on top. It was free; I don't know why for sure, but I am a frequent customer.

If I wanted to buy from the tamale or the ice cream vendor, I had to move as soon as I heard them calling from blocks away. By the time I got the wheelchair off the porch and rolled myself to the gate, they will have passed by my house if I waited too long.

When I returned from the vendor, there was a walking stick outside my door underneath the terrace roof, crawling upside down. I'm glad I knew it was a walking stick; otherwise, it would have scared me. Here in the tropics, with banana trees growing in the neighbor's yard, I'd have wondered what it was. I don't think I've seen one since my days at 4-H or church camp. I haven't seen many in my life, but they were so impressionable, you don't forget them. With six long spidery-looking legs, about four inches long, including the tail that stands up, it looked like a twig with legs. Here, it was essential to know your insects, so you knew which ones were harmless and which you needed to avoid.

It's 11:00 p.m., and I can't sleep, so I wrote a thank you note to Bob, a friend of mine in Mineral Point. It's a long overdue thank you for getting rid of the blue room in my life since he painted my bedroom in Mineral Point yellow last spring. My mother thought I would come back, even though I never said I would.

Today is an inspirational day, my birthday. When I have a birthday, it's celebrating that I didn't kill myself, did not choose death for another whole year. When I was in the States, I didn't want to live; if I can live in Mexico, I do. I will be visiting Mineral Point in August; there is a reporter there who wants to write an article about my travels despite my disability.

An Interview

35

WHEN I MET Mr. Janz, and he started to interview me, he asked me why I felt I was willing to go traveling by myself in a wheelchair. I told him my grandfather was a mountain climber who took risks. When he was thirty, he was struck and killed by lightning while climbing in the Alps. I probably take after him. I'm an adventurous person, too. But I don't climb mountains; I scoot around on knee pads. I need special equipment, just like mountain climbers do.

Mr. Janz said he'd found out from the ALS Society that I had been quite the activist in my earlier life and wanted to know more about it.

"To look at me now, you would never guess that I lived a full life of activism. Vietnam veterans coming home with health problems from Agent Orange, the defoliant used during the Vietnam War, inspired me to write a paper about my concerns."

"In 1984, although I was having balance problems, I was able to visit Barneveld, a town in Wisconsin that was devastated by a tornado, which killed nine people. Because I brought flowers to the residents every day for a week, they called me 'The Flower

ESTHER MARIA RITTER   140

Lady'" I dealt with people who were dealing with disaster and trauma; I knew I wasn't alone.

"Although I thought of suicide, I found an encouraging counselor who said to follow my dreams. I decided to trust in God and continue on my life's path. Priorities change when you know your time is limited. We plan for years, and then something unexpected happens, like an incurable disease. You don't fit in that world anymore. In Latin America, I felt I still did."

I told Mr. Janz how thankful I was to Ray Plankey, the director of the Cuernavaca Center, for letting me stay there for part of the last year. "He makes me feel that, foremost, I am a human being with a personality and joyful spirit."

I told him that the poor and disadvantaged were inspired by God to have dignity and self-determination, and that is what I saw in Nicaragua. "I could become obsessed with this disease and spend all my time looking for a cure," I said. "I don't want to do that. Am I going to do something meaningful with the life remaining or waste my time? Having a debilitating disease puts a deadline on your life. I have to make friends with death, not be afraid of it."

***

I suppose a mother should be a kind, loving person who wants the best for their children. A mother is not to be jealous because her children might have achieved something she didn't.

"How does it feel to be so special?" My mother asked me when I get attention from others, like the reporter.

"Mother, I'm having an awful time coping with this terrible disease," I said. How can she wonder how it feels to be so special?

When the Milwaukee Sentinel wrote an article about me, Mother didn't show it to any of her German friends in Milwaukee or Brookfield, Wisconsin. She visited them a week after the newspaper article came out. When I asked her if she showed them the article, she said, "No. We talked about other things."

I think my mother believed I was on an ego trip with this article. I felt obligated to do the interview when asked to show disabled people they can go on with their lives and be part of the world.

Consider an acquaintance of mine, a quadriplegic whose doctors recommended to her husband that he should have her institutionalized. He didn't, and now she has a full-time job at the university. Let us live no matter how deformed or handicapped we are. Let us take part in society.

36

Adios to My Friends and Mexico

THE TIME CAME when I returned to the United States for the last time. I never wanted to leave Mexico. Ray noticed I was having a harder time holding my spoon. Even when sitting in my wheelchair, I would slump over. He decided it was time to call my mother. She; Ruth, my sister; my niece, Heidi; and my nephew Willie came down to Cuernavaca to bring me home.

Ray arranged a goodbye party, and all my friends came to celebrate with me and say adios. Even Don Pedro; Mea; and my precious godchild, Maria, traveled from Emiliano Zapata. Mea brought me some pictures she had taken the last time I had seen her. One showed me sitting in a wheelchair by a horse. This picture represents how the disabled feel when not included in life. The second picture showed me on the horse with Don Pedro and Maria walking beside the horse to support me. This picture represents how, with help, the disabled can be a part of our world.

Upon returning to Mineral Point, I lived for some time

with my mother on Commerce Street and then later in my own apartment. I hired homebound helpers, who came to the studio. I stayed at home as long as I could. Mother came to live in the same apartment building, and her help made a world of difference to me. I had my list ready to use the help wisely and tried to be as independent as I could. Putting ads in the local newspaper for helpers, I found excellent support and met exciting people. It was always stimulating to talk with them and learn about their lives and families.

Having plenty of time to reflect on my life, I realized I was feeling weaker and closer to being with God. I was happy that, at my crossroads, I chose the activist's path. My experiences in Mexico and Nicaragua supported me in my life's struggle; we lived in solidarity with each other. I followed the road less traveled, and it made all the difference.

37

My Memories

AS I CONTEMPLATED my life, Orlando kept popping into my consciousness. I remember meeting Orlando in the South of France, in Cagnes-sur-Mer, a tiny village above the Mediterranean Sea. He was one of the strange men who came in and out of my life. We lived together for three and a half years. Eventually, he told me the story of his life.

AWOL in the Korean War at age nineteen, Orlando was held by the military at Riker's Island, New York City, on the East River between Queens and the Bronx. There he awaited his trial in prison, as he could not afford bail. He told me he escaped from Riker's Island by swimming across the East River but got caught in his underwear and sent back to Riker's. Nobody believed his story; I'm not even sure I did. Because of the notoriety of the escape, the other prisoners began treating him better. Before escaping, he had spent nine months in solitary confinement.

Orlando got to know some guards, who protected him from those who used to beat him. He was not a criminal; Orlando had been studying to be a surgeon when the government drafted him into the army.

"I went to Korea, at the point of a .45, and conveyed messages during the war," he said, explaining, "Because of my photographic mind, I didn't have to write the messages. I just memorized them. So if I were caught by the enemy, they could not get the message off my body or know I was carrying information."

When he came back, he spent over a year in the hospital, as he'd contracted encephalitis, a sleeping sickness.

In therapy, he tried painting; the artwork helped him heal. The doctors thought he might never recover. He went to the Art Students League in New York City. Even before that, he was drawing as a child. The professors told his mother when he was younger, about seventeen, that he had a fine line just like Leonardo de Vinci.

When I met him, he had already been out of the war for quite a while. He was living on his disability pension in the south of France, barely scraping enough together for a living. The positive that remains from the three and a half years was that I learned to picture and think visually. I watched him draw and paint and listened to his explanation of Goya, Cezanne, and Picasso. He admired them very much and studied their works, not the writings about their works, but the actual paintings of these artists, the strokes they made on the canvas.

I phoned his mother Estrella today, October 23, 1993, Orlando's birthday. It surprised me she had the same phone number.

"Orlando died one month ago," she said. "He was living in Puget-Théniers, France, a tiny village near Nice and Cannes."

I didn't register the conversation because I was in shock. My father died on October 23, 1978, on Orlando's birthday.

When I called him Orlando, I surprised Estrella because all of his relatives called him Roy. I felt special; he was Orlando to me. He gave me the most beautiful painting of his, The Toblerplatz. It is an abstract piece showing the energy and exciting life around the station where the streetcars met in Zürich, where we lived. The canvas shows lots of different shapes in vibrant colors of burnt orange, rose red, Prussian blue, sunshine, and gold yellow, as well as royal purple. It is interesting how the colors change and intersect and how the painting is so three-dimensional, like pieces of colored cellophane piled on top of each other. When I look at it, I have sweet memories of a cozy apartment we sublet for three months, in Zürich, Switzerland. What times we had together, going to movies, sitting at the coffee shop indulging in espresso as I watched him draw and paint. When I die, I would like this painting to be given to Estrella.

38

A Package from the Past

FOR A WHILE, I lived with my mother. But I eventually found a small apartment in a low-cost complex in Mineral Point, Wisconsin.

One morning, a large package was on the front stoop. My sister Ruth brought it in and helped me unwrap it. I recognized a painting made by my friend Odessa while we lived together at The Wooden Shoe. She had painted the fields behind The Wooden Shoe.

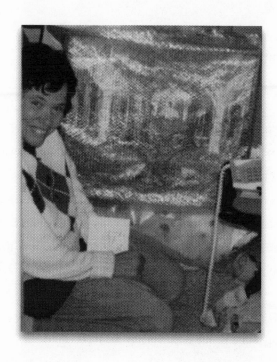

Editor's Note

I wanted to thank Odessa for the magnificent artwork that made Esther so happy with memories of the Wooden Shoe. I wasn't sure if she would have the same last name. The process of tracking her down proved to be quite a detective story. Researching the Wooden Shoe on the internet, I learned as much as I could about the people who made the commune their home. Thinking Odessa was an unusual name, I searched for Odessa on the internet. I found Odessa Piper, who founded a restaurant in Madison, Wisconsin, called L'Etoile, which emphasized environmentally-conscious cooking and dining. Intrigued, I read on, as The Wooden Shoe had stressed this concept back in 1971.

I discovered Odessa had likewise lived at The Wooden Shoe, so I was on the right track. Continuing to investigate, I found a website under the URL odessapiper.com. On the home page, a "contact me" button invited me to learn more, so I wrote to ask if she had known Esther and mentioned The Wooden Shoe.

She e-mailed me back, informing me she thought I might want the original Odessa. She had chosen the name when she'd migrated to Wisconsin after leaving The Wooden Shoe. The name had stuck when she worked in the restaurant business. Odessa didn't remember Esther, and we figured out Odessa had joined and left before Esther joined in the summer of 1971.

She remembered the original Odessa, with whom she had been in touch fifteen years ago. After reviewing her records, she found a phone number. I wondered if it would still be correct. I dialed. I was excited; this was the closest I'd been to finding Esther's Odessa.

The phone rang, and when a woman's voice answered I asked,

"Do you remember an Esther Ritter from your days at The Wooden Shoe?"

"Yes, I do," she said.

"I am Esther's sister-in-law, Judy Ritter. I am looking for the Odessa who painted a picture of the fields behind The Wooden Shoe, which Esther received a few years ago."

"Yes, I sent that picture," Odessa replied. "I remember how much Esther liked it."

"She loved the vibrant colors," I said. "Every time Esther saw the picture, lovely memories of you, Rain, and her Wooden Shoe family came back to her."

"You are welcome, and thanks for telling me how much it meant to Esther," she said.

We spent part of the afternoon sharing Odessa's recollections of the time she spent with Esther as a family in the early '70s at The Wooden Shoe.

Odessa permitted me to publish the picture in Esther's book. Thank you, Odessa. This picture brought so much joy and comfort to Esther in her final days; it deserved to be on the cover. The path in the painting represented Esther's path of activism throughout her life, despite ALS.

The Ritter family gave this picture to me when Esther died; I will cherish that painting for the rest of my life.

I promised, Odessa when Esther's book is published, I will send her a copy of Esther's book.

Epilogue

ON OCTOBER 1, 2005, Esther died, surrounded by her family. We had been feeding her little chips of ice, as in the last stages of Lou Gehrig's disease, there is a strong chance of choking if given a large amount of water. She knew she was dying. She begged me, her sister-in-law, to not call her sister Regina, who lived in California and was planning a vacation to Europe. It was hard explaining to Esther that I couldn't do that. I told her Regina would never forgive me if I didn't call her. Esther and Regina were close, and she had the right to be there. Regina postponed her European trip and arrived in time to spend a little time with Esther and tell her goodbye.

On a lovely fall day, where the colorful leaves under your feet crackle and the sun shines to accent the red maples, we had a memorial service to remember Esther.

Many friends and relatives remembered her fondly as a woman who took charge of her life, despite her disability. We all agreed she had lived a life of compassion, respect for diversity, and a deep sense of social justice. She was a woman who never lost her deep interest in politics or foreign policy.

One of Esther's friends said her last hurrah was to plan and organize a Peace March for a July 4, 2005, parade to protest the war in Iraq. Wrapped in a peace flag, while her neighbors cheered, she felt like an activist again, and that is all she ever wanted.

How to honor the memory of such a woman? We should never take our health for granted. Find ways around what seems like insurmountable obstacles, don't give up, and follow our dreams. Esther's wish would be for us to carry on her legacy and work toward a more just and peaceful world.

Regina's Tribute to Her Sister Esther

AS I REFLECT on Esther's life, I think how much our part-time farm life in Oak Creek, Wisconsin, may have influenced her. Living on twenty-seven acres, the five children had lots of room to roam. Esther loved going to the far end of the property into the woods to explore. Mother always had a reasonably large garden, where she planted vegetables from seed and got us involved to some extent with planting and hoeing. I think Esther may have gotten her interest in organic gardening right here at home. We had some alfalfa fields, wheat, and oats, as well as chickens and five goats on the farm.

Already in Sunday school, Esther seemed to like to discuss ideas about religion and philosophy. This activity continued during her life and may have come from our father and mother's many discussions. I recall Esther's sense of adventure as she traveled to and worked in Lake Tahoe, living on the Nevada/California border. She would send us pictures of her small Volkswagen parked against a massive granite wall of rock or a plowed wall of twelve feet of snow.

Our uncle in Switzerland arranged for Esther to be an au pair and mother's helper in the French part of Switzerland.

There she had the opportunity to ski and improve her French, which she had studied in high school and at the university.

Often Esther would say how glad she was that she had not been disabled all of her life. She at least got to have the experiences of skiing and hiking. She especially felt sorry for children who never got to do these things, if disabled at a young age.

In the 1980s, Esther was living in Mineral Point, working first at the Hodin Center and then at Lands' End in Dodgeville, Wisconsin. During that time, she made her first trip to Mexico and knew she must return.

Around 1983, Esther began to notice some problems with her legs as she went downstairs. She had some other balance issues also. It took the doctors some time to diagnose the problem. As the disease progressed, Esther kept making adjustments. She used construction knee pads to get around and get up and downstairs. For a long time, Esther was able to use a walker. I remember when she rented a wheelchair and had it sitting in the house to get used to the idea of using it one day soon.

Jan, a friend of Esther's, encouraged her to go to Mexico, even though she used a walker and sometimes a wheelchair. Esther and Jan were involved with the Peace Council of Wisconsin. Jan knew the director of the CCIDD in Cuernavaca. Esther was invited to become involved in bringing groups from Canada and the United States to educate others about the roots of poverty and oppression in Latin America. The center invited campus ministers, pastors, and teachers for one or two-week programs to help them understand the social, economic, and political realities of poverty within a Christian faith dimension. Esther enjoyed meeting and talking with people as they educated each other.

Later, Esther got an apartment in Cuernavaca. Those days in Cuernavaca were the most special for Esther. She even became the godmother for a young girl, Maria de La Paz, whose family became close to Esther. In later years, the family hosted Esther on a visit to Mexico for one week. Esther loved speaking and hearing Spanish. She managed to visit Nicaragua while she was in Mexico, which had been a lifelong goal.

In the past five years, Esther had been at the Mineral Point Care Center. Although she didn't travel outside the country anymore, residents of Mineral Point, Wisconsin, would often see her going around town in her Rascal Scooter, with the orange flag sticking high in the air. Here she is "snowmobiling."

In 1999, Esther received the Outstanding Self Advocate Award from the Arc of Southern Wisconsin. Self-advocates exercised their rights by representing themselves. They had a part in all decisions made in their lives and in policy decisions that affected them.

The
Arc of Southwestern Wisconsin

1999

OUTSTANDING SELF ADVOCATE
AWARD

Esther Ritter

During this time, Esther was on the Commission on Aging, she continually educated herself about the Medicare system and the rights of the disabled. She was active with phone calling and follow-up letters to assemblymen and congressmen.

In 2003, Esther received a letter from Ron Kind, Wisconsin congressman from the 3rd district in Wisconsin, in response to her letter. She had written a letter, concerned about President George W. Bush's decision to commit United States' troops to Iraq. Mr. Kind also sent Esther a letter that fourteen politicians, including himself, had sent to the president concerning postwar Iraq. They expressed the need for an international reconstruction program to help Iraq achieve prosperity and reintegrate into the global community. Esther cherished this letter as a symbol that she was still an activist.

We will all miss hearing her opinions on many subjects and interests in the world. Mostly we will miss her bright eyes when she hears something unusual and her hearty laughter as she enjoyed friends and family.

I like to think of her in heaven, united with her mother and father—free of ALS, walking or running, no longer confined to a walker or wheelchair. Or, more likely, after a short stay in heaven, she would ask to come back to earth. Considering Esther's commitment to helping others, she might be somewhere in this world, serving the poor and disadvantaged, an activist for eternity.

Printed in the United States
By Bookmasters